When the astronauts go to space, they don't just hop on the shuttle, fire up the motor and say, "Let's check out earth's orbit." They have a checklist. For too many years, entertainers and musicians have either not bothered with or been talked out of tending to the business that is a part of a career, whether you care to deal with it or not. Thus, the road to and from success is littered with far more wreckage, caused by lack of a checklist, than there are those who make it across the finish line.

Livingston Taylor has been teaching this fact to students and "want to be's" for over two decades, and I have been honored to have participated in a few of those sessions. When I first read this book after its first publication, I immediately thought to myself that we, performers of my generation, had no tool like this to use as our guide to the stars—and what a wonder "checklist" it is. Even with the onslaught of technology, the basics in this book still apply. If you are going to attempt to jump through the hoop of shameless show business, buy this book, study this book and use this book. You just might make it to the planet of your dreams.

— Jimmy Buffett

I love Liv's advice to young musicians, which applies to actors, painters, virtually all artists: Hypnotize them with rhythm and seduce them with discipline. Every great work of art has its own innate rhythm, its own music, which is to be honored even if it's dealt with freely and inventively. In his **Stage Performance**, he teaches us how to attain that important theory. It's a wonderful read.

— Blythe Danner

A personal, entertaining, and extremely informative account of the art and craft of being on stage, told by a master storyteller.

— Jon Landau

STAGE PERFORMANCE

Livingston Taylor

mentor

An Original Publication of Mentor Publishing

Mentor Publishing
715 Boylston Street, Boston, MA 02116

Book design: Judith Krimski, Krimski Design & Illustration, Quincy, MA

Photos:
Front cover: © 2009 Philip Porcella
Back cover: © 2007 Bill Ewen (*stage photo*)
          © 2009 Albie Colantonio

For information:
Mentor Publishing
715 Boylston Street, Boston, MA 02116

ISBN: 978-1461068846
Printed in the U.S.A

For Gail,
who always remembers to love.

Introduction

Acknowledgements

To Maggie Taylor, whose personal and professional advocacy, rapier wit and bulldog tenacity dragged me across a thousand finish lines and rescued my career.

To Charlie Koppelman, whose love of the great song and affection for me kept me afloat through my grim late twenties and early thirties.

To Don Law, whose unshakeable moral compass and sense of fairness have allowed him to sail successfully in some very rough show business seas, for giving me a first-hand view of what happens on a storm-tossed deck.

To Donna Roll, a teacher whose technical knowledge of voice is coupled with a complete understanding of the underlying heart and soul that drive the need to sing.

To Rob Rose, the unofficial mayor of the Berklee College of Music, who brought me into the classroom because he believed I might have something to teach.

To Shelly Schultz, the quintessential agent who softened the harsh lessons of show biz with a secret stash of love and compassion.

To Nancy Fitzpatrick whose good humor, patience, and uncanny ability to decipher my handwriting have made this project not just possible, but one of my more pleasant experiences.

To Dan Beach, my best friend and keeper of the flame.

And to Julie Roper, who was willing to herd cats until this rewrite was good to go.

With special thanks to Betty Fulton for the exceptional management that keeps my world spinning.

LIVINGSTON TAYLOR

Stage
Performance

Introduction

I've always been curious. Why is water wet? What keeps a plane in the air? Why does glass shatter? Why is stone hard? Why does gold shine and iron rust? I've spent countless gentle hours thinking about gravity and how it might be controlled. And I'm at my best when I'm straining to observe it all—squishy earthworms, gray-green moss, lightbulbs, bacteria, doorknobs, paramecia, firebrick, mushrooms, faded wood, indelible ink and bamboo. Born a camera, I am always photographing my instant of consciousness. That curiosity brings us to this book.

I teach a performance class at Berklee College of Music in Boston, a school that's been in existence for over sixty years and is well known as the foremost jazz and contemporary music school in the world.

The random nature of my class (not to mention my life) convinced me that the only way to organize this book was to collect a semester of tapes of lectures to an actual class. It has been something of a distillation process to get those into print. I have left them in the order in which I found them, which is to say, this book is the unfolding of a semester's classes. Although there is a vague outline, I'm content to let each class follow its own course. Rather than force the book into some rigid framework, the chapters spring from the moment. Reading from front to back is fine, but feel free to let it fall open where it may and dig in.

I love being around my students at Berklee. Twenty something is a great age—just aware enough to have the entire mountain range in view, and energetic and innocent enough to believe it can, in fact, be crossed.

Let me introduce you to thirteen students who together will represent in a single class the students I've had over many semesters. They are Jason, Kathy, Boris, Arnold, Charlotte, Laura, Dustin, Krystal, Jennifer, Lee, Trevor, Tim and Phil. They are composites of the two thousand or so students I have taught over the past twenty-plus years, and they will allow us to explore some of the issues that arise, semester after semester, in the exploration of stage performance.

As the "semester" progresses, you will get to know these students in more detail. For now, understand that they represent the most diverse assemblage I could imagine in one place at one time. Students arrive at Berklee from all over the world, from all economic and educational backgrounds, with one thing in common: a consuming desire to have their musical and philosophical ideas heard and recognized. They've been told by everyone who loves them that there are easier paths to walk. Some eventually will have to take the easier path, but right now, they need to explore the limits of what is possible. I am both honored and excited to help them try.

I call my assemblage of students a class, although that's not quite accurate. It's more of a laboratory where, for three classes—two hours apiece—each week, we experiment and explore what it means to present yourself and your vision to other people.

This book exists because so much information flies around the class that it's impossible to take it all in at once. I want my students to have something to refer to long after the semester is over and as their careers evolve. I also want others—anyone intent on developing their confidence before an audience of any kind—to have a place to turn, and to hopefully find some help in the ramblings of a veteran performer.

CHAPTER ONE

What Is a Performance?

I was sixteen years old and in genuine trouble. The chaos of my brain was crashing into the demands of ordered functional society, and the situation was causing enormous pain. I was at war with school, a battle that had begun years earlier when I was forced to repeat third grade. As a result, my study habits were nonexistent, my grades were terrible, and I wound up in an alternative high school west of Boston where the doors were locked and the students had no keys.

Music has always been a large part of my existence. Early on, I found sanity in the discipline of rhythm and the order of chords and melody. Singing is, by some accounts, organized shouting, and the organized shouting of song and lyrics wicked away much local pain.

I recall, as though it were yesterday, the instant I realized music was going to be my way out. It was a clear, cold early March day, and I was in transit. My status in the "school" had risen to the point where I was free to move between buildings unescorted. En route, I took a moment to look up into a painfully blue sky. The clarity of the day drifted into my thoughts.

Whenever I've gotten in trouble, I've been able to float above myself and somewhat rationally peer over the horizon into the future. On that clear March day, as I looked down at my situation from that lofty position, I realized academia wasn't an option. I was 130 pounds soaking wet, with occasional asthma, so physical labor seemed a stretch. Yup, no doubt about it. Music was going to be my way out.

So I went back to my dorm room, picked up my guitar, and went to work.

More than four thousand performances over more than forty years, sixteen CDs, hundreds of songs, acting jobs, TV hosting, commercial singing and writing, and just about every other

3

experience in show business have given me a few thoughts on what's happening out there.

I ask my students, "What is a performance?"

Arnold says, "It's when you play onstage."

Jason says, "It's going in front of people and doing what you do."

Jennifer says, "It's entertaining people by showing them your talent."

Those are good answers, but they all indicate that a performer is doing something *to* an audience. I don't view it quite that way.

Rather, I think of a performance as a conversation between you and an audience. A conversation based on listening, with the knowledge that the best conversations are the result of *taking in*, as opposed to *putting out*.

There's a world that exists independently of your presence. Sounds, lights, people—there is an entire space that functions quite well without you. It is necessary to see and understand that which already exists to know what contribution you can make. Good performance is based on what actually is, not the fantasy of what you hope will be.

A performance is a conversation that begins when you go onstage, take in all that's happening around you, get a sense of where you are and how you feel, and then react to that reality.

Since it is a conversation, there will probably be a response to what you do—although there are no guarantees, as you'll see. If the audience likes what you've done, do it again. If they don't, do something else. Of course, sometimes it's impossible to tell if they like it or not. Heck, sometimes even the audience can't tell.

Don't worry about this confusion. This book is about having belief in yourself, developing confidence in your ability to have the conversation, and learning to be free of fear and open in front of all those people.

"Now, listen. What do you hear?" I ask the students.

"Traffic."

"A bass from another classroom."

"Ventilation."

"Voices in the hall."

All of the external noises are as much a part of a performance as anything else. They are always present in varying degrees. Listen to the noise that already exists and think of how you can adjust your own noise so that it fits in with the environment.

To acclimate yourself to the externals, take some time onstage before you begin a performance to listen—again, taking in before you put out. In other words, notice and pay attention to everything that's happening around you. First, be patient. Don't let nervousness jump-start your performance and force you to begin before you're ready. Breathe in. Breathe out. Wait. Watch your audience. Listen to them. Be still. Patience and stillness are very inviting rooms.

I love silence. I'm a connoisseur of silence. And the most important thing about silence is not that the audience can hear you, but that *you can hear them.*

Sometimes their communication is quite clear: "Yo, bucko! You stink! Get off the stage!" But usually, they communicate displeasure with more subtlety. However they do it, they send continual signals, and if you're lucky, there will be enough silence around to hear what they're saying.

Remember the acronym K.I.S.S.—Keep It Simple, Students (my adaptation for this purpose). I always try to play simply enough so that I have plenty of room to respond to the unexpected outside stimulus: people entering the hall, a spilled drink, a siren in the street. In shows past, a distant train whistle has prompted a quick verse of Johnny Cash's "Folsom Prison Blues," and the sound of that nearby siren has prompted me to suggest I should leave NOW—both are good for a quick laugh.

Room to react tells an audience that you're in the moment and that you are sharing the moment with them. I always watch my audience, and when the lights are in my eyes, I listen to them: the rustle of corduroy, the creak of a chair, the cough of boredom. All are part of the conversation of performance. I strive to speak fluent "audience-ese." When it is really quiet in an auditorium, I can whisper onstage and be heard by the people in the top balcony as though I were next to them.

Please remember: Silence is the canvas on which we paint.

My job onstage is to look and to listen, to identify problems and, whenever possible, to solve them. Sometimes I'm the right guy in the wrong place, and nothing I do works. For that particular audience, I will be terrible. It happens sometimes.

When I'm onstage, my top priority is not technique, style, or passion. My top priority is to perform with total awareness of my surroundings. I'm watching and listening all the time because I need information from my audience. How are they doing? Are they okay? It's my job to pay attention to them. I need their support to survive. To them, I'm a quality-of-life decision. To me, they are my employers and patrons. They deserve and will receive my complete attention.

If you're an amazing singer, songwriter or instrumentalist, you may not have to worry as much about your audience. Your talent may shine so brightly it will more than compensate for any lack of audience attention. But you need to ask yourself, "How good am I? Am I good enough in one area to ignore weaknesses in other areas?" I don't know about you, but I'm not good enough to be commercially successful firing on seven cylinders. I need all eight.

There are performers out there who take beautiful care of their audiences. A while back, I attended Jimmy Buffett's concert at what was then known as the Tweeter Center, in Mansfield, Massachusetts. Jimmy had sold out all four nights with twenty thousand people in the venue each night—a total of eighty thousand people, at an average of thirty dollars per ticket. That's right, $2.4 million gross in ticket sales. Wow!

Now is Jimmy Buffett great looking? Is he a great singer? He's had strong Top 40 radio airplay ("Come Monday" and "Margaritaville"), but that may not be the real key to his success. So what is it? This is what I think: he's having that conversation with his audience—all the time. A give-and-take. He sees them, and he knows that his success is dependent on their freely given goodwill.

I was there on the third of the four nights, and at one point during the show, Jimmy looked out at the crowd and said, "Last night, I thought we had gotten just about as crazy as we could get. But, darn, you people are about to prove me wrong!" The crowd went wild. They went wild because Jimmy made them feel important. He made them believe that they had a direct influence on the course of the show—that their enthusiasm, under his watchful eye, would be of great value in the show's success. Whenever he performs, Jimmy keeps a watch on his audience. He smiles at them. He is genuinely concerned that they enjoy themselves.

When he walked onstage at the beginning of the show, he surveyed the crowd and then welcomed them. "Good evening, everybody," he said slowly.

("Liv, the larger the crowd, the slower you talk," Jimmy once told me.)

"It is so great to be . . . back . . . at the Tweeter Center." Here, there was a slight pause, at which point Jimmy breathed in and said, "in . . . ." Now the audience was totally on edge. Did Buffett know where he was? Of course he did, but he wasn't quick to relieve the tension. He formulated exactly where he was and double-checked it in his mind before he spoke. Finally, he blurted out, ". . . Mansfield, Massachusetts."

There was relieved, ecstatic pandemonium. Why? It's simple. Because Jimmy could accurately identify his exact location, as opposed to a vague "the Boston area" or "New England." This told the audience that he was completely aware of his location, and it allowed them to abandon their reality and enter his. Because he was able to prove that he knew exactly where he was, it seemed reasonable to let him captain the ship.

As a performer, it's easy to believe that you are the reason why people are enjoying themselves. After all, each of us is pretty important to ourselves. As individual performers, Livingston Taylor, Jimmy Buffett, Alison Krauss, et al., are actually minor catalysts around which an audience builds an experience. People will see that Livingston Taylor (or Jimmy Buffett or whoever) is playing at a local club on Friday night. Carol and Sam will get together with Jack and Betty, get in their car, have dinner, and go to the show. The performance was the catalyst for getting together, but our part in their evening was certainly less important than their time together as friends. On their way home, they'll discuss the performance, whether it was good or bad, better or worse than a previous time. Maybe my voice was a little scratchy. Maybe I was a bit tired in the beginning. As I said, we're a major part of our own lives, but a remarkably minor part of the audience's.

Please remember: Your audience means a lot more to you than you mean to them.

N-e-r-v-o-u-s-n-e-s-s

Stage fright is as old as the stage itself, and many of the most famous and successful in all fields have suffered and continue to suffer from it. Let's explore it a little.

I ask my students if any of them get nervous before they perform. Every hand rises except Dustin's. He explains he's too nervous to raise his hand.

I ask, "What does it feel like to be nervous?"

Kathy says, "I'm short of breath. I have a stomachache. I have to go to the bathroom. My knees shake, my palms are sweaty, and I've forgotten what I'm supposed to do."

When you're nervous, where is your focus? Who are you thinking about? Are you thinking of your audience, the people you're working for? My take is that when you're badly nervous, you're thinking about *yourself* and the discomfort you're in. This is the problem with nervousness. It takes your attention away from your audience and forces you to be self-centered. You're thinking about yourself when you're being paid to think about them.

I try to think about all those Jacks and Bettys and the nice evening I hope they are having, and how much I want them to enjoy what's coming next. In other words, I focus on someone other than myself. Even though I am not yet on stage, I try to pay attention to my audience. Once I'm on stage, my attention turns to the conversation, so that any fear I may have had dissipates as I lose my self-centeredness in my attention to others.

Let's look even closer. You get nervous because you're afraid and worried you'll make a fool of yourself or that something unexpected will surface and put you in a situation where you'll be out of control.

"Why do people get nervous? What's the worst that can happen onstage?"

Jennifer says, "You can be really bad. Terrible."

Arnold says, "You completely forget your part."

Trevor says, "Your zipper is down."

So it's the fear of humiliation and failure. Sometimes the worst does happen, and in spite of your best efforts and wishes, you wind up being *absolutely awful*.

I want you to know I've been absolutely awful many times. I've played onstage where the entire audience booed me at the top of their lungs, sometimes simply because I was the right guy in the wrong place.

How does it feel to be absolutely awful? Let's qualify it. "What's the common phrase that people use to describe being terrible onstage?"

Phil responds, "'I died.'"

In spite of how it feels, has anyone actually died from being terrible onstage? Not that I've heard of. So let's figure out how bad it really is so we know what we're actually going to face. Have you ever stubbed your toe? Hard? You're in stupefying pain for a couple of minutes. Have you ever broken a bone? Yes? It hurt and inconvenienced you for weeks or months.

Well, I've stubbed my toe hard plenty of times, and I've broken both arms and a leg (the result of a raucous childhood). Being awful onstage is worse than stubbing your toe really hard, but not as bad as breaking a bone. It hurts, but you get over it, and the damage isn't likely to be permanent.

Being fearful of being "absolutely awful" is obviously detrimental to your performance, but how do you get out of it? As we've already discussed, you've got to see your audience with every sense available to you. And the reason why you pay attention to them is to respect the fact that they have given you their time and money. They want to share your view of the world, and they need you to be in the moment. They want to feel as though you are speaking to each of them as individuals. Now these are probably decent people who will be sympathetic and supportive if they see that you are in distress. But they want to have a good time and to suspend their reality and enter yours. To laugh, to cry, to be part of the reality that you, as an entertainer, are creating. They want to believe you are glad to be with them.

This is why nervousness is a problem.

If you take attention away from your audience, there is no conversation to be had. Just envision trying to speak with someone who has headphones on and their eyes closed. The conversation doesn't get very far. Their attention is a gift. Don't throw it away. Even if you think you don't deserve it, receive that gift graciously. "Thank you for your energy. Your presence is a beautiful compliment."

I've heard it suggested that one should visualize the audience in their underwear or some other compromised, embarrassed state to mitigate nervousness. But making yourself feel better by the degradation of others is rarely successful. Your audience is a treasured gift. Treat them accordingly.

Jennifer remarks, "I use my nervousness to pump me up for a gig. I love the adrenaline rush!"

Jennifer, I know that feeling. When I was younger, I often used that adrenaline to push through my nerves. The problem I found in using that type of energy was that I often missed the people who needed my music the most. The ones that are heartbroken, hurting and searching for a lifeline of humanity tend to be gun shy and need to sense stillness and compassion before they can join. If I'm driven by adrenaline, we might miss each other.

Earning a Living

Now let's talk about another essential ingredient in your career. I ask the class who would like to be a professional musician, singer or actor.

All hands rise.

What comes to mind when you hear the word *professional*?

Boris says, "It's what somebody does for a living."

"Professional—for a living." This phrase indicates that someone is getting paid, that they are making m-o-n-e-y. If your music isn't making money, it will become your hobby. If your art can support you, you'll be able to spend most of your time doing what you love—making music, creating your art.

Before we go further, let's define what money really is: money is a mutually agreed upon item of value that makes life convenient. It is not bad or evil. It is simply *value given for value received*. For our conversation here, the exchange is payment for performance. It's possible to do a show where all ten members of the audience are so pleased that they invite you to their houses for breakfast the next morning. The problem is, you have ten offers and you can only eat one breakfast. What's the solution? Eat one breakfast and let the other nine people give you three dollars each so you can grab that Egg McMuffin on subsequent mornings.

One of my students asks, "Livingston, what are the chances that I can make a living making music?" If your needs are simple, your chances are good. If you're looking for externals to fix a broken inside, there will never be enough.

In the performing arts, where does the money come from? What is its ultimate source?

Lee says, "Record companies."

Tim says, "Club owners and promoters."

These are true enough answers, but not completely accurate.

You'll find great fantasies at work when you think of how you'll achieve success: "If I could just get a big manager to hear my music...," or "If I could only get a record company to sign me...."

Have you had similar fantasies about your life? Sure. You have them all the time. I certainly do. "Darn. If I could just get discovered,

I'd be home free. If I could only get that one big break." Have you tried that one on yourself? I have. I've seen the knight in shining armor coming to rescue me from myself.

I want to give you the bad news right away. In all likelihood, you're not going to be discovered. It really doesn't happen very often. There are exceptions here, but in reality few are ever "discovered" and rocketed to fame. From a distance it may appear that way, but on close examination, you'll see that successful careers are actually a mix of lots of hard work, intelligence and talent (okay, and maybe a skosh of luck).

The source of all money in the music industry is *the audience*. The audience is the marketplace. It is made up of individuals who have decided that your art has value, that the reality you create on stage is attractive enough to deserve support. First, their support comes with their time, and later, with their money—CD sales, downloads, concert tickets. Record companies, managers and agents, although important, do not generate income directly. They actually take money from the audience, keep some and pass the rest on to the artist. Their value is a conversation for another day. The only enduring source of support for a career is an audience. They pay your salary. They are the foundation of your career.

So now we get to the essence: *how does one develop and care for an audience?*

Your career is neither a lottery, nor the product of random chance. What your career is—and what it will be—is the result of the cultivation, care and feeding of the people who pay your salary: your audience. The good news is that you don't have to be discovered. Showing up each day, working on your art, and being clear and observant will carry you.

Your career is in your hands, and making it happen is a doable deed.

Do Something
One of the main things I want to emphasize is the idea of flexibility—

not waiting for things to line up properly, but moving ahead with what you've got right now. I like controlled movement, even in the wrong direction. Parts that move don't rust and freeze. At the risk of being dramatic, a phrase I like to use is, "We may die moving forward, but we will certainly die standing here."

There is no rule book for your career. It's going to be made up as you go along. So don't get lost in a fantasy of how your career should be. Have your heroes and your influences. These are wonderful beacons to follow when the road gets dark. But your career will not be Madonna's or John Coltrane's or Phish's. Nor are their careers necessarily as wonderful as you may believe. Remember, you're seeing them through the distorted filters of the entertainment media (*Rolling Stone*, MTV, etc.). You're also going to hear a lot of rumor and supposition about how various people got where they are. Just don't expect to follow their path. Celebrity information drawn from mass media is notoriously incomplete, and truth is often a minor barrier to a salacious story. You don't really know about these artists' careers. You can and should admire and critique others, but your career, by its very nature, will be unique to you.

Let the Performance Begin

Since a good conversation often begins with an introduction, the first thing I have my students do is introduce themselves around the class with an appropriate exchange of names and a good strong handshake, all the while maintaining eye contact. After that, I have them step onto the stage at the front of the room and introduce themselves, one at a time.

A student introduces himself, saying, "Hello, my name is Trevor."

(Trevor is a lanky twenty-year-old with long hair and tight pants. He is a guitar major with Bon-Jovi-type rock-and-roll dreams. Unexpectedly alone without his guitar, he flushes with fear. His body tension reminds me of frozen cardboard.)

"Where is Trevor looking right now?" I ask.

Phil says, "At you."

"Why is he looking at me?"

"Well, you're the teacher."

Yes, but I am also just another member of Trevor's audience, even though it probably is a good idea to shoot a glance my way. I am, after all, passing out grades at the end of the semester. But what about the rest of the crowd? He should be looking at them and trying to actually see them. Looking at the audience is the most basic way of telling them that you're paying attention to them.

As we continue the introductions, I ask the class to pay close attention to the person onstage. A performer sends out signals and messages. And the audience sends back to them messages and makes continual decisions about them. Literally volumes of nonverbal communication are going back and forth every instant: the tension of the arms, the tilt of the head, the depth of breath, the closeness of the shave, the cut of the clothes. These and thousands of other cues are instantly transferred to and absorbed by the audience.

Laura balks. "I don't judge people by a first glance," she says.

I try to explain the difference between judging and responding. Let's walk down the street. Each person we see generates a response in us. The business person's clean-cut suit, the carefree flow of a student released from class, the oblivion of a chatty group of close friends, the alarm and sadness triggered by a street person passed out at an odd angle in a doorway. Judgments based on first impressions are not bad. It is responsible behavior. That said, hopefully we have the capacity for reassessment as more information about a person becomes available.

I'm amused by the arrogant reporter who demands to know why a voter did or did not support a politician. When forced to make a verbal response to nonverbal information, it's often painfully simplistic. "Uh, I don't like the way he cuts his hair." This prompts outcries of supposed voter ignorance. Nothing could be further from the truth. The spoken part of our reaction to other people is small indeed, and I believe that people are remarkably capable at collecting nonverbal information, and wise in their assessment of their fellow humans.

In the delivery of nonverbal information to the audience, I ask the class to follow a predictable order:

1. Walk onstage.
2. Face the crowd.
3. Find a spot where you're comfortable and well lit.
4. Be still and see your audience.
5. Say your name. (This is the performance.)
6. Be still and look at the audience. Make sure they received what you gave out.
7. Bow slightly.
8. Accept applause, if appropriate.
9. Leave the stage.

I ask the class, "When Trevor was in front of you, did you form opinions about him? Of course you did."

Every person we see conveys, in a split second, a dictionary's worth of information about themselves. This is not to say our opinions of people can't or won't change, it just recognizes that first impressions are inevitable.

In all the time that you're onstage during this fifteen-second introduction, saying your name is the only verbal component of the performance, and it takes up only a couple of seconds. Yet in spite of the brevity of the "performance," you have imparted a huge quantity of information to your audience.

The introductions continue.

"Hello, my name is Kathy."

"What did you learn from Kathy during that introduction?"

Arnold—a good-humored Brooklyn, New York, native—zeroes in on her accent: "She's from the South." The class is much amused that with his own distinct accent, he should remark on hers.

Did any of you notice how Kathy walked onstage and kept moving? How she never stopped? Never took a moment to be still?

More than anything else, stillness is essential to establishing control. Stillness is the straight line, the horizon from which all the angles and curves of a performance flow. Stillness allows an audience to observe you and become familiar with your externals. Once comfortable with the outside, the chances that they'll accept what's on the inside improve.

Being onstage is like playing a grown-up game of Simon Says. If you are tense, your audience will be tense. If you are still and at ease, your audience will be still and at ease.

Remember, people love to suspend their reality and enter another's. If your reality is nervous and agitated, it will exhaust them. At some point, they'll have to turn away to rest. As your panic level rises, it can be seen and read by your audience, who see rigid shoulders and arms, shallow breathing, wide eyes, a clenched jaw. All these things say you are ill at ease. Conversely, if your arms and shoulders are relaxed and your breathing smooth and steady, it will tell your audience that you are comfortable in their presence.

Lee, a trumpet major from Taiwan, raises his hand with a most concerned look. "Please, Mr. Taylor, does this matter for me?"

I think yes, absolutely. The rules of engaging your audience apply regardless of the instrument played. From operatic singing to the washboard, you must be still, look and observe—taking in before putting out.

An important component of nervousness is expectation—that is, what might happen? Let's see how much trouble we can get into with expectations.

"Who has had the experience of rehearsing in their rooms, thinking that their music sounds pretty good, only to get onstage and have it completely fall apart?"

All hands rise.

It's amazing that the same piece of music can be so good in one place and so terrible in another. It's no wonder performers get nervous. They never know when they are going to be blindsided. Here's what happens. Performers in one environment develop a series of expectations about what will happen elsewhere. They carry those expectations onstage, and when a show doesn't go as expected, panic sets in and the house of cards crumbles.

Expectations and assumptions are like tree stumps in the dark. They are ready, willing and able to help you stub your toes. It is terrible to panic onstage. You get offstage. You cry. Your friends, other than the ones who snuck out the back door, tell you that you weren't that bad. That means you were pretty bad. Then your mother tells you that you weren't that bad. Guess what? That means you were absolutely awful. Let's find a way to stay grounded in ourselves and avoid panic.

An expectation is a resentment waiting to happen. Hope is a totally different animal. It is so sad for me to see artists ratchet down their hopes to avoid the pain of unfulfilled expectations. Let me give you an example from my own life.

I recently recorded a new CD filled with brand-new songs. I was, and am, very proud of the project and was delighted to have such a quantity of music flow through me. Before the sales figures became known, folks would ask how well I expected the CD to sell. I would respond that I hoped it would sell ten million copies. Eyebrows often arched at my hubris. Indeed, actual sales were much less than I had hoped. Bitterness? Never! My hope was for the moon. My expectations were more than met by the opportunity to create.

Resentment is the price of unfulfilled expectation; a gently broken heart is the price of all the hope in the world.

Please remember: we asked to be in front of an audience. An audience has the right to reject what we offer. And we have the right to let that rejection break our hearts.

It is tough to believe that you have the right to be onstage, that you have the right to be still and at ease until your surroundings are evaluated and you are ready to proceed. To believe you have this right doesn't come overnight. I've been at it for more than forty years, and I still struggle with my right to be onstage.

The moment you walk through the door of the place where you are going to perform, you send out signals about who you are and what you are about. You cannot turn yourself on and off. You are a continuum.

In the early part of my career, I struggled more often with my right to be onstage. It's surprising where the permission came from. It was in the fall of 1976, and my career had been in a downhill drift since the disappointing sales of my most recent album, *Over the Rainbow*. With no record contract and shrinking audiences, I was beginning to have serious doubts about whether I should remain an entertainer. The light at the end of the tunnel was faint indeed. Then one afternoon, I got a phone call from a fellow named Ian Anderson. Ian is the head of a British group called Jethro Tull, with whom I had toured extensively in the early 1970s. Ian asked me a favor. He was not feeling well and had two sold-out shows to do at Madison Square Garden in New York City. He wanted to know if I would be the opening act for these two shows. I was complimented he had chosen to call me, but I told him I had reservations. It was my sense that his audience had become quite rabid over the years and that they would probably kill me if I were to attempt, as the opening act, to delay their reunion with their favorite band, Jethro Tull. However, remembering my financial situation, I asked Ian what he would be paying. The reply: $1,000 a night. With a stack of unpaid bills in clear sight, my mind changed easily. I'd be there that afternoon.

Showtime came, and the Garden was packed. The announcer said, "Ian Anderson isn't feeling well. Please welcome Livingston Taylor." He was trying to be informative, but he inadvertently threw me to the lions! As I stepped to center stage, alone with my guitar, I was greeted with a chorus of boos so thick, low and aggressive, I thought the noise would drown me. So there I was, a guy at the end of his career, being booed by sixteen thousand chemically altered, predominantly male adolescents. In the midst of that din and self-doubt, a remarkable thing happened. As I played my first song and accepted the reality of the audience's displeasure, a calm and clarity came over me. I was onstage, and I was ready to be there. I belonged there. That sixteen thousand people adamantly disagreed made no difference. It was their problem. I could see and hear their clear disappointment with my presence, and although it made me sad that they were saying no to what I had to offer, it did nothing to change the fact that I was where I belonged. *They* were in the wrong place, not me.

It's taken a number of years of hindsight to be able to articulate what happened that night. At the time, my response was harsher. As the boos rose to a climax and the clarity came over me, I stopped playing, looked at the audience, and spoke clearly into the microphone. "Ian Anderson and Jethro Tull are here tonight. In about twenty minutes, they're going to be out here, and they're going to be *fantastic.*" The crowd went wild. "But right now, I'm here, and if you don't like it, you can *get the f—k out.*" Oh, boy, were they mad. Nonetheless, I finished my fifteen minutes.

When I got offstage, Ian Anderson came up to me and remarked that my show had been a pretty tough go. I agreed with his dry English understatement. Knowing that we had one more night of this, and in an attempt to reassure me that the worst was over, Ian explained that the next night would be easier because the second night was the second show that had gone on sale. Certainly, the fans would be less rabid. You can predict what happened. The second night was, in fact, the *first* night to have gone on sale, and when I hit the stage, they were ready for me. The opening boo was a third again as loud as anything I had heard the night before, and this audience added a couple of twists. As I was playing my first song, a sparkle to the right caught my eye. It was an empty whiskey bottle on its way to the stage. It smashed, and the glass drifted around my feet. Tull was so popular at the time that they had sold the seats behind the stage: 360 degrees of people committed to kicking a little folk heinie. A longneck beer bottle floated through the spotlights, missed me by inches, and went into the audience in front of me. Simultaneously, a cherry bomb exploded in the deep left side of the hall.

Now I had a problem. My presence onstage was putting my audience at risk. In spite of my feelings about them, which at that moment were quite negative, they were, nonetheless, my audience. As such, they were my responsibility. That my presence was putting them in danger was intolerable. I broke my rhythm, stilled my strings, looked out at them and announced that it was impossible to continue. After a quick bow, I left the stage.

From that low point, my career fortunately ticked upward with a major record label contract and some good solid public acceptance of the music I was making. It's drifted up and down many times since

Madison Square Garden, but always with the sense that, for better or worse, I've earned my right to be onstage.

The students continue their performances—introducing themselves and dutifully following my prescribed order for being onstage. After the names, I have them follow the same routine by reciting the alphabet. After ten minutes or so of the alphabet performance, I explain that despite the sophomoric nature of the exercise, their recitation of the alphabet is, in fact, a real performance and that in spite of its simplicity, large quantities of nonverbal conversation are taking place between the performer and the audience.

Phil asks plaintively, "When are we going to get to play our music?"

I respond, "Not as soon as you want, but soon enough. Probably in a couple of weeks. But be patient. I want your performances to stand on a solid foundation, and it takes some time to understand what that foundation is all about and to be comfortable with it." I explain that these early exercises are teaching us how to build the frame that will surround our unique creativity. "Your assignment for next week is to memorize one or two minutes' worth of prose or poetry and be ready to recite it."

Their sighs are music to my ears. Although skeptical, they tell me that they are willing to listen to and—for the time being—follow my vision of performance.

CHAPTER TWO

Crawl
then Walk

Even though we've been through it in the first week, I want to reemphasize the most important issues to be sure they're gotten through before we move on. So I open the class with a question—"What is a performance?"

"It's a conversation between an audience and a performer," someone responds.

"And who pays a performer's salary?"

"The audience."

"And why does an audience give a performer money?"

"Because they want to."

Yes. And, I don't mean money as in a guitar-shaped swimming pool. I mean money as *value given* for value received.

I ask, "Have any of you seen any big shows recently?"

"Tom Petty. Phish. U2. Steely Dan."

"Ooh, Steely Dan at Harbor Lights? Were they good? Good sound and lights? I would guess they played all the hits. And how about the crowd? Sold-out, I bet?

"Was Jeff Baxter there, playing guitar? If you're not sure, he probably wasn't." I know Jeff well. In the early 1980s, he coproduced an album for me, and he likes to make his presence known.

"How many people at Harbor Lights? Ten thousand? All paying an average of twenty-five dollars per ticket? What's the gross on that? Yeah, $250,000. Hello! That's a lot of cake."

What can Steely Dan afford, if they're grossing $250,000 a night? Great travel and food, super sound and lights, roadies to set up and break down the stage, lighting and stage designers, limousines, and lots of rooms in good hotels. In short, they'll have plenty of money to finance a world-class tour.

"Now, what can club owners or promoters expect to make from you guys? What are your names presently worth?"

Phil says, "Not much," shaking his head.

Sadly, at this early point in your career, it's true. Because you have yet to develop an audience base, your names are worth little to a promoter. And because of what you can earn, which is almost nothing in comparison to acts like Aerosmith, Dave Matthews Band or Billy Joel, you have very little power to demand much from club owners or promoters. You need to expect and prepare for marginal sound systems, cranky club staffs, crummy and sometimes nonexistent lighting, low pay, and generally indifferent treatment. Without an audience to finance you, your power base cannot help but be small. Don't fret. Rather than lamenting the situation, let's figure out how to work with what you've got and how to make that audience grow.

The very fact that an artist is on MTV, VH1 or Top 40 radio means they've developed a strong power base. That's good for them, but don't be confused. They are not you.

As I've said before, your career is unique to you. It doesn't matter how Elvis, Billy Joel or U2 did it. You can be influenced by, emulate, and admire them, but don't compare yourself to them. Understand that their careers are not yours, and that trying to design your career after watching them or anyone you admire on MTV or in any other performance venue is like trying to build a house after looking at a lightbulb.

The nature of the business dictates that your career gets made up as you go along. Flexibility and adaptability will be your keys to success. Wishing about an unknown future is a monumental waste of time. It's much better to spend time observing and learning to respond appropriately.

As we've discussed, your career is not what you *put out*. It's not in fancy guitars, weird haircuts or big breaks. It's not what goes out, but what you can *take in*, and what you do with that information. Your eyes, ears, and senses of touch, taste and smell all plug into your greatest career asset: *your brain*. This is where your career and success come from—not from your heart, your soul, your makeup or your instrument, but from your ability to process what's happening around you and to realistically assess where you are and what you have to work with. The ability to adjust will be a repeating theme throughout your career.

Making Do with What You've Got

In the late 1970s, I did a tour with Linda Ronstadt, a wonderful singer and a good friend. On this tour, she brought a Hammond B-3 organ that she used on one love song. She was making enough money to go ahead and absorb a refrigerator-size piece of equipment for one song. Doodads are difficult and expensive to carry. They require the kind of time and attention that can distract you from your boss— your audience. You and I do not have those resources, but we do have brains, and we need to use them.

When I travel and do shows, I am usually alone, and one guy can only carry so much gear. So I like to use what's around me. If you go camping, you can either bring fuel and a stove with you, or you can bring a pack of matches and just pick up sticks, strike a match, make a fire—and, using what's already there, cook that hot dog.

Please remember: Stay lean and simple. Avoid gimmicks. Concentrate all your resources on building an audience base.

Who Are You?

When I play, the first thing I do is show up early and introduce myself to as many people as I can—sound people, wait staff, janitors, bartenders, anyone remotely connected with the show. I tell them my name and explain that I'm the person scheduled to play that night.

Say your name early and often. Names are important. If people don't know your name, how will they find you again, to buy your CD, come to a show or tell their friends about you? *Never* assume that someone knows who you are. You will embarrass them and eventually yourself.

Early on in my career, I did a few shows with the rock group Emerson, Lake & Palmer. At the sound check before our first show, there was a person playing piano. Was it Keith Emerson or a roadie? I didn't know, and he didn't introduce himself. It made me feel awkward and worried. In my unsettled condition, I made a promise to myself: I would never assume that somebody would know who I am. I always introduce myself.

There is a well-known TV personality in Boston named Liz Walker. Although we've known each other for many years, our paths cross infrequently. Every time I see her, I reintroduce myself, and she always exclaims with exasperation, "I know who you are!" I'm delighted she does, but I still don't leave it to chance. Name confusion has prime embarrassment potential.

One time, I was working at Folk City, a now-closed club in Greenwich Village. I was exhausted, and my brain wasn't working too well. During my sound check, a familiar-looking face came into the room. When I got through, I approached the person and introduced myself. He identified himself as Jackson Browne. At the time, I had not met Jackson, and the resemblance between the real Jackson Browne and this guy—combined with my fatigue—made the introduction plausible. I was taken in by the charade for probably thirty minutes. When the truth came out, I felt foolish and embarrassed. The person told other people about my confusion, and it left me with much bad feeling. It also created in me a strong commitment to avoid embarrassing other people whenever possible.

Please remember: Embarrassment is an invitation to resentment.

This can be expanded in many directions, one of which is not to admonish people in a loud, public voice. If your criticism is inappropriate, you'll be the fool. Even when it's accurate, if others can hear the criticism, you not only run the risk of humiliating the person you're trying to correct, but also being seen as disruptive yourself. Any potential improvement in their behavior could be diminished by their resentment.

Before my show starts, I make a point of getting out of my dressing room and circulating through the crowd. (Given the atmosphere of many club dressing rooms, this is not a particularly difficult decision.)

Out in the crowd, I shake hands, introduce myself and smile. I feel like a politician, and actually I am. I am out campaigning for the continuation of my career. I'm running for Top Ten. I love finding an excuse to visit the people waiting in line to get into my show, shake their hands, look them in the eyes, and tell them how glad I am to be with them.

I ask the class, "Who here has met someone famous?"

Laura says, "I met Tom Bergeron in the airport last week." (Bergeron was then host of *Hollywood Squares* and more recently has hosted *Dancing with the Stars*.)

"And so, from now on, you have a personal connection to him. Correct?"

"Yes."

When you meet audience members, they develop a vested interest in your success. If they have already paid money to see you, you know they must already like you some. Let them feel they can get to know you. Go ahead and *work that crowd*.

I was in Japan a couple of years ago, and my Japanese promoters were apoplectic when they found me mingling with the audience before my show. They were worried for my safety, but also worried that I would ruin any cachet that I might have by showing myself to be just like everyone else. But the people in the audience were my employers. They had hired me by buying a ticket. I needed to see and touch them to make sure they were all right, to take in as much information as I could about the environment in which I was preparing to place my music. As my promoters became accustomed to my style, it became less of a concern and more a source of amusement.

No One Showed

Everyone knows what to do when you're playing to a sold-out crowd that thinks you're the greatest thing since shoe polish. But when the crowd is small, you and I are faced with three problems. First, there is the sadness at the size of the audience. Second, the financial reality is that that the promoter hasn't done very well. Last but not least, there are the people in the audience—the fifteen or twenty people in the 150-seat club—who are worried. They're thinking, "Maybe I've made a mistake in coming to see Livingston. Maybe my taste isn't so good. Am I a chump for liking this guy?" Or they're thinking, "Oh, how awful for him when I like him so much, and how hard it must be to play to so few of us." This is where showbiz gets hard. Can I go onstage and face my sadness at the size of the audience and, at the same time, feel gratitude and love for the people who are there? Can I forgive myself for not drawing so well? Here, I fall back on the difference between hope and expectation. I always hope for the sellout audience jamming the hall, but my expectations are met by a single listener.

Can I come up with a way to spread the financial loss around so the promoter will want to work with me again? The answer is yes—and by doing so, I probably lengthen my career. I've never had trouble giving back a little money to a promoter who has taken the risk to bring me to his or her venue and who has offered me full pay when they have lost money. It seems only fair to lessen the blow somewhat. It allows the evening to end on a gracious note. Grace under pressure will dictate the length and quality of your career.

Get Comfy

It's important to stay within yourself, whether you're performing or not, but particularly when you perform. If the intent is to put the audience at ease, you must be at ease. Be sure to do material with which you are comfortable. Your career is not happening yesterday or tomorrow, but right now. The more time you spend in the past or the future, the less you'll have to spend in the present, which is your career.

Boris asks, "Do you ever put yourself out on a limb with a song?"

Yes, but not far out. When I introduce a new song in my show, I make sure I know the song well enough to play it well. I just play bits of it at first, and I open my eyes and ears and watch and feel. How is it going over? How do I feel when I am playing it? Can I sell it? Do I believe it? If I don't like the way it's going, I segue into something else. Because I work alone, I have this flexibility. If you are working in a larger production, your ability to change quickly is obviously reduced. However, you can and must be able to change as situations warrant.

Kathy asks, "How long does it take you to learn a song or a routine?"

For me, it can take years to learn a song, because it goes beyond learning the words and music. It's learning the song so well that I can quickly adjust, twist or shade it to the demands of a specific audience.

Jason says, "I do a lot of cover songs. When I do my own songs, I like to tell people about them."

I usually avoid doing that. If the song doesn't move people, who cares where it came from? I've never heard anybody ask about a song they didn't like. If the song has moved them, they will find out about it.

I also avoid telling people what a song is about. Early on, when asked, I used to tell people what I had in mind when I wrote a song. I found that my reality invariably underwhelmed them. Today, if someone asks me what a song means, I turn the question back to them: what do they think it means?

After they've told me their fantasy, I say, "Wow! That's amazing. That's just what I had in mind." They are delighted. Occasionally, I will tell an audience the circumstances surrounding a song: the why, the where and sometimes the when. The who and what I leave for their imagination.

Poems, paintings and songs mean different things to different people. If my song has moved someone, I let the song mean to them what they want it to mean, not necessarily what it means to me. The reality of your song is rarely as exciting as the audience's fantasy. The song may have imprinted itself on them with a memory that has nothing to do with you or your reason for writing it. A really good song holds something different for everybody.

While we're on the subject of songs, let me mention what I think are the important ingredients for a hit. The great pop song doesn't make the artist sound good, it makes the listener sound good. Singing the great chorus in the shower or cranking the volume during a slow commute—the best pop songs make every would-be singer sound great.

As we move into the performance part of this class, Trevor reads a poem by Edgar Allan Poe. I have him reread the last half. As he does, I turn off a fan that I have left running in the back of the room.

"Do you hear the difference it makes to have that fan turned off? It's a rhetorical question. . . . It makes a big difference."

White noise—that is, the constant sound of air-handling or refrigeration units, traffic, or a generator—is destructive to a show and deadly for a performer.

White noise limits our dynamic range. It masks casual conversation, and worst of all, white noise makes it impossible to hear the subtle noises an audience uses to communicate with the performer.

The creaking chair, the crossing of legs, the cough—they're the sounds of someone who's bored shifting in his or her seat. These are very soft sounds. Some audiences are far more emphatic: "Yo, broccoli face! Get off the stage!" But generally, the signs of an unhappy audience are fairly quiet. White noise makes you deaf to the quiet grumbles of discontent. If the bright lights have already taken away your eyes, you are going to need your ears. When I go into a club or concert hall, I pay serious attention to white noise and eliminate it whenever I can.

The sounds of cash registers, blenders and other human-operated noise generators in a club are invasive but intermittent, and therefore not as corrosive as the steady hum of an air conditioner or refrigeration unit. I generally ask the "powers that be"—the theater managers, club owners or sound engineers—if it would be possible to turn off any air-handling units when I am onstage. If I explain the difficulties to them, at least they know there is a problem in their facility. Some are completely unaware of such issues. But be warned; they often balk, so when it comes to a choice between putting up with white noise or getting paid, go ahead and compromise. Don't let principles burn you alive. Live to fight another day!

Most amazing to me are the sound companies that set up amplifiers onstage with cooling fans that sound like coffee grinders. These people are hired to reinforce sound. Instead, they pollute the environment with their own white noise. Perhaps it's that they have heard the noise for so long that they no longer register it. Tread gently if you mention such things, particularly if they are running your sound for the evening.

I have played brand-new, expensive theaters where the designers have paid surprisingly little attention to their air-handling systems and have seriously diminished their theaters with white noise. In spite of the millions spent, they will never be the best places to give or receive a performance. It's so sad. There is a lovely theater out on Long Island that renovated its air-handling equipment. When the job was done, the new equipment was so loud that the theater was really not suitable for performance unless the equipment was shut off.

Air-handling equipment must be large enough to handle volume without velocity. Theater designers, if you're reading this, I beg you to think of this when you design a multi-million-dollar performance facility. You can lose much of that value by trying to save a few thousand dollars on a ventilation system. The fancy sound system won't bail you out. Increased amplification *cannot* compensate for lost silence. And while I'm on the subject, let me say to all you teachers out there, listen for white noise in your classrooms. Attempting to teach over the hum of ventilation will force you to speak in a voice that is exhausting to you and brutal for your students. To teach effectively, the classroom *must* be quiet.

Unfortunately, few people are familiar with true silence, and when we find it, it often scares us. The world is an increasingly noisy place—with TVs, computers, cell phones, iPods, and the need to communicate 24/7. We are raised in boisterous homes, go to schools that are filled with sound, move to a noisy dorm, and live lives that include a busy family and, most often, a job in a noisy place. We rarely experience silence. If you, as a performer, are comfortable with stillness and silence, you will be able to lead your audience through this unfamiliar environment. And, my friends, there is nothing more wonderful than complete silence in a sold-out hall—the anticipation of the paint on canvas. Let me say again—silence is the canvas on which we paint.

Phil has a question. "In the places that I play, the audience cheers for the baseball game on the TV. How do you compete with noise like that?"

"That's a great question, Phil. First, when we book dates, it is often helpful to know whether we are booking in the middle of the World Series or on Super Bowl Sunday or even in high school basketball season."

My agent often will remind a promoter of these things as she sees them, in order to try to maximize the audience. If I do encounter the competition from a TV, I try to think of it not as a competition, but as a whole entity. We're not here to grab an audience away from something else. We're here to make sure they're doing okay. It's sad if they can get more entertainment from a TV screen than from us, but it's okay. They're the boss. It's their choice to make. I want an audience to have a good time no matter where that good time comes from. I observe that there is a ball game going on, and that some members of the audience are going to be drawn to that. If I have noticed the TV in the room being on before the show, I might ask that the sound be turned off for my show, but it may not be. The ball game is part of the show, and I can't change that. I can only hope that my music will draw in the crowd. If enough of them are trying to listen, maybe they will deal with the cheering from the bar, but it's not my call to make. I will be ready for them if and when they're ready for me. It's important to me on many levels that I'm ready. However, being ready doesn't mean you're going to be called.

Please remember: It's sad to be ready and not be called. It's tragic to be called and not be ready.

There is always an ebb and flow to an audience and a show. Sometimes you have to let them go, wait your turn, and then reel them back in. Be patient. Ask yourself, "Where can I add to their enjoyment?" If they need to make noise, you might try getting quiet. If they can entertain themselves, let them. It's better when an audience comes to you out of attraction and need rather than trickery and gimmickry.

An analogy I like to use is that of somebody spearfishing. Thwack! The fish is speared and hauled in close. There's only one problem. Although it's close to you, it is either mortally injured or dead. That's okay if you're hungry, but hardly helpful if you're looking for a long-term relationship. We want to base our relationship with an audience on mutual attraction, not spear-and-retrieve.

Absorb the environment. Be patient and take your time. The hardest thing to realize as a performer is how much time you have. Where is the audience going to go? The answer is "nowhere," unless you *drive them away*. As I've said before, this is a big game of Simon Says. The audience has hired you to take control. They want to enter your reality. If you are still, they are still. If you are tense, they are tense. If you are at ease, they are at ease. If they trust you, they will put themselves in your hands.

Bands often go onstage and yell, "Hey! How's everybody doing tonight?" Do you get the feeling that they actually care how the audience is doing? When they yell, "How are you doing?" maybe they're really saying, "I'm panicked—please tell me how I'm doing," or maybe they're saying, "This is the last chance you're going to have to be heard by me." The audience crosses its collective arms and says, nonverbally, "Why don't you open your eyes and see how I am doing? Don't demand my time and money and then force me to tell you how to take care of me."

Everything you do onstage will tell a story about who you are and how you feel. You cannot hide. If you try to hide, you look like you're hiding. That tells a story, too.

As we move to the performance portion of the class, Jennifer, an earnest brunette from Tucson, Arizona, comes onstage to read a short prose piece. Although she's fairly thin and small, Jennifer displays a stillness and sense of purpose that demand attention. When she gets to the end, before there is any applause, she says, "Thank you."

I question the timing and placement of the thank you.

After an audience applauds, it's fine to thank them. However, too often people use "thank you" as a signal that their performance is over. There is an easier, clearer way to show an audience that you are through. When you get to the end, be still and take in the effects of what you have put out. Finally, take a *slight bow*. A bow breaks the spell. It is the universally understood signal that a segment or the entire performance is over. Then, if they applaud, it's fine to thank them for their gift.

In your early career, when people are unfamiliar with your music, they need to be told when the end is at hand. If you neglect to tell them, they won't know. Have you ever felt the insecurity of not knowing whether an unfamiliar piece was over? Worse than that, have you ever applauded loudly at the wrong time? It is most embarrassing. Don't ever leave an audience uninformed. Let them know when it's time to respond, and when they do, thank them. As I said, their applause is a gift. And remember, receive it graciously, whether you think you deserve it or not.

Krystal, a tall, statuesque African American, is the next person to perform. She has had professional modeling experience, so her presence onstage is quite arresting. She asks, "Livingston, do I have to have my piece memorized?"

"Not necessarily. Let's see what happens if you read the piece instead of memorizing it." Krystal does this and it sounds fine, but there's one problem. When you read what you perform, your eyes are on the paper and not on the audience. As a result, your attention is diverted from them. So, it's fine to read if you must, but I believe that audiences are paying you to pay attention to them. Anything that takes your attention from them is going to cost you.

At this point, in thinking about attention, I can't help but reflect on Krystal's appearance. For people who are incredibly attractive, it is often difficult for audience attention and interest in you as a performer to go beyond your looks. They may never see what's on the inside, having set in concrete a fantasy based on the outside. But being beautiful doesn't confine you to being taken at "face value." You have to use your appearance to show *care for your audience*. Show true compassion. So the audience can say, "She's beautiful, and she's paying attention to me. Wow."

Please remember: In the long run, your audience will support you—not because of what they see in you, but because of what you see in them.

Kathy, who has a sweet, girl-next-door country-western vibe, is the next to perform. As she speaks, her Texan accent soothes and amuses the class. She does a nice job, but she also does something common to newcomers on stage. She wiggles. She is in constant motion. This could be just nerves, or perhaps the theory that a moving target is hard to hit.

Remember, as I've said before, performance is a big game of Simon Says. People suspend their reality and enter yours. Periodically, you have to be still or you will exhaust your audience, and they will have to turn away to rest. You must allow them places to rest and regroup, and they can do that only if *you* rest and regroup.

There is a big difference between being still and being rigid. At this time in the lecture, I demonstrate and then ask the class to join in an exercise of leaning forward and back, allowing our arms to be totally relaxed and to swing and fall at will.

"It makes you all laugh to see me go forward and back with relaxed arms, doesn't it?" I ask. Relaxed arms are funny. They tell an audience that you are at ease. When you go from relaxed to being tense, it creates contrast, and that is good. Tense to tense? No contrast. Boring.

Arms are a great indicator of comfort. Loose arms are relaxing and funny to an audience. Mary Tyler Moore, Steve Martin and

Richard Hunt, who played Grover on *Sesame Street* and the Muppets, are very good at this. Some people are so comfortable onstage that you will buy any plot they are selling. Bill Murray and the late, great Muppeteer Jim Henson come to mind. They are so relaxed and at ease that no matter how ridiculous the premise, you will bite. Their total comfort is irresistible. You will willingly enter their reality. This is a great gift.

Why Would Anybody Want to Go Onstage?

People who are well-adjusted and secure don't normally turn to the performing arts as a career choice. Lawyers, teachers, engineers, plumbers, and homemakers are the career choices of the better adjusted. Being in the performing arts is so difficult that if you didn't have to do it, you probably wouldn't.

Sometimes a lawyer or a doctor will approach me and express their desire to be onstage. I'm bemused by their innocence. They don't understand that people who write, paint, dance or sing do so not because they want to (in spite of what they tell themselves) but because they must. Nothing else seems to fit.

I believe that people in the creative arts had a sense, an inkling, a vision, when they were nine or eleven or thirteen years old, that they might be a creator, that out of the ethers of an unseen universe they might pluck the familiar and make it appear in an unexpected place. They had the sense that people would be wowed by such magical feats, that the clear cool water of the creative process would be well received by an eager crowd thirsty for the wizard's magic. I believe that art is the expression of the human spirit. As such, it is the highest level of the human experience. Creators can be found anywhere a human being is straining to find and perfect a better way.

You want to be a performer even though you know there are easier career paths to choose, like the steady work and health care benefits found in a big corporation. Instead, you're willing to go it alone in the cold, dimly lit world of the performing arts. You didn't choose to be here. Nobody does. You are here because you're driven. As a group, we performers tend to be insecure and rather hard on ourselves—demanding more of ourselves than we can reasonably deliver. These are states of mind that can cause us big trouble. They make us nervous and fearful, driving away the very audience we so badly need. At this point, I need to descend into some psychobabble, and I want to apologize in advance.

I see most life situations as falling into four distinct steps. Using the familiar environment of driving a car, let's go through them.

One: *action*. You're driving along the highway, and out of the blue, somebody cuts you off. It was unexpected, and it scares the bejesus out of you. The fear triggers a huge adrenaline rush, which throws you into state number two.

Two: *reaction*. Words are spoken, harsh stares exchanged, predictable hand signals given. Adrenaline, fear and rage are in full swing. This is a very *dangerous* place to be. Events are accelerating and can easily move out of control. This is when people say and do things they often later regret. As time passes, you start to calm down and you move to the third state.

Three: *acceptance*. Along with acceptance, there is often sadness. There is the heartbreak of the hand you've been dealt, the unfairness of life. "I'm just driving along, minding my own business, and this maniac cuts me off. I could have wrecked my car. I could have been killed. What kind of world are we living in? People are turning into terrible drivers. What a crummy day." Although painful, this state of sadness is actually quite safe. The sadness of acceptance has replaced panic, and now we're starting to heal and preparing for our complete return to sanity as we enter the highest state of the human condition.

Four: *forgiveness*. "We're both okay. I've driven that way myself sometimes. I've been out of control in the past, and others have cut me slack." Have you ever looked in your rearview mirror after inadvertently cutting someone off? After the initial surprise, you cringe in anticipation of the expected rage. You screw up your courage and glance in the mirror again, and when the person you've almost hit shakes their head, visibly sighs and looks slightly away, it's clear that they're letting your trespass slide. You are forgiven. The total relief that comes from being forgiven, or from forgiving others, allows life to move on.

Let's see how these four steps relate to being onstage when the circumstances in which you find yourself do not fit your preconceived fantasy.

One: *action*. I walk onstage, and the environment bears no resemblance to my expectation.

Two: *reaction*. The unexpected, unfamiliar environment is overwhelming me with panic, nervousness and fear, and I become completely self-centered. Will I remember my lyrics? Will I pass out? Will I make a fool of myself? Am I going to throw up? I am devastated by falling so short of my lofty expectations.

Three: *acceptance*. After the performance, I eventually accept the reality of what happened, and it makes me sad. The experience wasn't what I expected or hoped for. I was not good. I might even have been the worst I can possibly be—absolutely awful. I desperately wanted to be good, and I must accept the fact that I simply was not.

Four: *forgiveness*. I did the best I could with what I had. I accept responsibility for what happened and for the audience's decision about me, and I forgive myself.

By way of review, when I am nervous, it's a signal to me that I am fearful and out of control, that I am in the dangerous reactive state. What am I scared of? I'm scared of being awful, being embarrassed, making a fool of myself. Instead of staying in this dangerous place, I simply move ahead. I allow myself to feel the total heartbreak that I would feel if my fears came true, if I were truly "absolutely awful" onstage.

We've already discussed the fact that audiences do not want your fear or bitterness. They have plenty of their own. The question is, will they accept your sadness? The answer: an unequivocal yes. Audiences don't mind sadness and contrition because sadness and contrition can be healed by compassion and love. And human beings do enjoy the power to love and forgive.

It's okay to be human onstage, to forget lyrics, to sing wrong notes. Not only do audiences forgive your humanness, they love it.

They love you to be normal, to make a mistake, acknowledge it, smile, shake your head slightly, forgive yourself and move on.

The ability to forgive is very attractive. When an audience sees that you can forgive yourself, they make the assumption that you can forgive them, too. That makes them comfortable, and comfortable audiences are happy to pay your salary.

Jason, a shy northern Ohio native, walks onstage, introduces himself, and gives a short explanation of what he's about to do. There's a problem. Everything he says sounds like a question.

When each? Phrase you speak? Sounds like a question? It forces an audience? Into a state of tension? And *drives them crazy*. They want to be told, not asked—informed, not quizzed.

It is said that this kind of intonation originated in California in the 1980s with "valley girls." It appears to be extremely contagious and already somewhat generational, and I think it needs to be addressed as a manner of speech that indicates a basic level of insecurity. It tells me the person needs constant affirmation from their listener. Audiences are normally filled with good, decent people who, if asked, will give that affirmation to the person onstage. But if they've received nothing before they are asked to give, it turns the giving process into a one-sided chore.

The performances in class continue with poetry and prose readings. Some students have a natural charisma, others virtually none. Although charisma and looks provide a slight advantage when you first step onstage, like "talent," they present their own sets of problems and can be vastly overrated. The quality of performance is contingent on what you can *take in*, not what you *put out*.

Please remember: Tenacity trumps talent . . . always. As we've discussed, the problem with talent and good looks is that you become used to people coming to you. Ultimately, careers are sustained by your ability to go to them. This is why the talented and the beautiful often work at a disadvantage, when compared to the tenacious and the fortunate.

So one of the keys to your success lies in making your audience comfortable. Of course, you hope for the best to happen, but if the worst should happen—if you are absolutely awful—you are fully capable of accepting the audience's judgment, and, although your heart is broken, you are also capable of forgiving them and yourself. Of course, it's easier to say than to do. Trust me, I'm still working on it. Wish me luck.

CHAPTER THREE

All Things in Good Time

I n any group, the question of leadership, when not clearly defined, is at issue. In a musical setting, it is crucial that a leader be identified. So I pose the question to the class: "Who is the leader of a band?"

Boris answers, "The lead singer."

Lee is convinced it's the arranger. Charlotte says it's the person doing the solo.

"Nice thoughts, people, but I had something else in mind."

I think the leader of the band is the person who holds the time, the person who has the best rhythm. The person with the *best rhythm* is the person to whom you return to get your bearings, to settle down, to reconnect.

Rhythm and time are the elements that allow you to be hypnotized. Ticktock. Ticktock. Ticktock. You are under my spell. A strong, even rhythm tells an audience that you are in control, that they can safely abandon their reality and enter yours.

Once you've committed your performance to predictable time, you must not break it. If, for whatever reason, you have "timus interruptus," you are in big trouble. Interrupting time is the signature of panic. More than anything else you say or do, interrupting time tells an audience that you are out of control, that things are falling apart and starting to fray at the edges. Their response will be to leave your reality and reenter their own.

Rhythm provides safety. It is the foundation on which we build our performance. One, two, three, four. One, two, three, four. One, two, three, four. Provide strong, even and confident time. Time predicts the future. After three beats that are strong and even, all successive beats are predictable to *infinity*. The audience feels this and surrenders completely. I offer you Ray Charles as an example. Listening to Ray Charles is like falling into a feather bed. His time is so perfect, so confident, so dependable that after the required three beats, you are totally enveloped and free to let go completely. "Yo, Ray, you drive." The singer Martin Sexton has a similar talent.

Good time speaks for itself. Now, let's talk about bad time and what makes it that way.

I say to Phil, "Do me a favor and snap your fingers." Phil starts snapping.

I stay on him, saying, "Okay. One, two, three, four. One, two, three, four. One, two, three, four. Right on the beat. Now keep it up."

Forty seconds pass.

How is Phil doing? Is he falling apart? Yes? Why?

Why is the time falling apart? It's crumbling because his fingers are getting tired. The lactic acid is building up, and the muscles are starting to burn. They ache. They cry for relief. They demand his complete focus. He forgets the crowd. He forgets the music. He loses the thread of the conversation. The fatigue wins, and in spite of his best efforts, the time falls apart.

You cannot hold rhythm externally. It must be internalized. Once the time is inside you, you can give it to any part of your body that you want. Sometimes you sway or tap your right foot and then your left. Maybe you turn your head or push a shoulder forward and back. If the time comes from within, it will show up on the most rested, comfortable outside part: hand, foot, eyes, hip or head—they all trade off. As one part becomes tired, another takes over. Watch people sway during Carnival in Brazil. Watch a Zulu or Native American dancer. Their time is internalized, effortless and completely joyous. They can keep it up for hours. People, this is going to be coming soon to a body near you.

If you are in time and at ease, the audience stays put. They are yours. If you lose time, they become uncomfortable, and the thread is gone. So find a way to be comfortable. Now, I can read your minds, and I know you're thinking, "I don't need to keep time; that's what the drummer's there for."

To the class, I ask, "Has anybody here ever played with a drummer who couldn't keep time?"

All hands rise.

Never abdicate time to the drummer or a piano player. It is everyone's job to hold and internalize rhythm. It's wonderful to immerse yourself in a blistering guitar solo or vocal "riff," and then, when you come back to earth from your journey, there are your bandmates, welcoming you back with the strong, even rhythm they've been keeping in your absence.

The conductor holds the baton. Watch the tip. Up, down, side, side. Up, down, side, side. One, two, three, four. The change in the baton's direction represents *the moment in time that is the beat*.

At a distance, the baton's movement looks sharp and crisp. The time seems pretty good. But up close, under a magnifying glass, does the direction of the baton change? Does it get ragged and dull? Is it early or late? Does the beat get a little loud or a bit tentative? Great time is even and predictable. The discipline of perfect time allows an audience safety with the most intimate detail of the human condition. Time is like the subway platform that allows us to stand inches away from the certain death of the raucous, roaring subway car.

What do you do during all the time that is not the beat? The greatest benefit of sharpening your rhythmic focus is that during all the space that is not the beat, you can rest. You can prepare yourself for that next moment in time that is the beat. Remember Simon Says. They'll be resting with you. Often, they will be ready for the next beat before it's time. But you are in control and will not be rushed. The beat will be delivered when necessary, and not an instant before. When you finally deliver, the audience will be completely receptive and most grateful.

For me, one person that exemplifies this concept of "focus and rest" is drummer Russ Kunkel. His focus is so sharp that the listener is hypnotized by the anticipation of the next beat. To paraphrase the old wine commercial: Russ Kunkel will serve no beat before its time. You must rest. You must have time to be still and renew yourself. If you don't rest, you cannot sustain the energy. You become strained and fall apart, and so will your audience. For self-preservation, they turn away.

So, let's review. How do you hold attention and rest at the same time? By focusing on the instant in time that is the beat. The greater the focus, the more time there is to rest. The more you rest, the more comfortable you are. The more comfortable you are, the more comfortable the audience will be. And we know what comfortable audiences will do, right?

I have a core within me that is the beat, and I send that beat to different parts of me: feet, fingers, hands, face, shoulders, hips and belly.

A great way of learning how to internalize time is to march. I love marching. It is God's way of enabling us to internalize time. Find a groove and live in it. Ticktock. Ticktock. Ticktock.

It's amazing when you consider the external things people depend upon to maintain rhythm: a metronome, the enthusiastic time-keeping of a bar crowd, or most commonly, the accelerated rhythm dictated by nervousness. How fast can I play? Get those fingers to top speed, and that is the time. Please do not depend on a metronome or other externals for time. A metronome is like life support. Though occasionally very handy, it is not conducive to a flexible lifestyle.

Again, time must come from the inside. Practice internalizing time. Many forms of repetitive exercise work well here: walking, running or swimming. Try this. Count off. As you walk down the street, count your steps in groups of four. Breathe in for four steps, breathe out for four steps. Or hum a simple melody that's in time with your steps. Try this, too: tap out syncopation against a predictable rhythm source—windshield wipers, turn signals, a washing machine out of balance, a blinking yellow light, or anything that is repetitious. Only after you become fully comfortable, after the time is established, then and only then can you start to place notes, chords, melodies and lyrics. Time is the foundation, and the foundation must be strong for the house to stand. Once you've established your rhythm, look at your audience. How are they doing? How do they feel?

Arnold asks: "Livingston, what are we looking for? I feel sort of stupid just staring at a crowd."

"Arnold, you're not really staring. You're watching your music land, looking for people who want to have a conversation with you."

A smile, a nod, a slight move that tells you they're with you. The music, lyrics and rhythm are the conduit through which the nonverbal communication goes back and forth. It is the framework in which an intimate conversation is possible.

Now that you've got your rhythm established, go ahead and dance a little dance. You heard me. *Dance.* People may laugh. If you dance like me, they definitely will. Don't worry. Laugh with them. Let them see that you can forgive yourself for being goofy.

The attempt can bring great pleasure. Clearly, Berry Gordy Jr., of Motown Records, understood that a little choreography and dance paid huge performance dividends. If I had my way, all performers would be in dance class for at least half of each and every day. Never be afraid to bust a move.

Please remember: A performer in a dance class is a performer interested in success.

Play the Hand You're Dealt

Boris is the day's first performer. He's a curious, outgoing twenty-two-year-old from a suburb of Munich, Germany. Clear-eyed and friendly, he tackles Otis Redding and Steve Cropper's "(Sittin' on) the Dock of the Bay" a cappella.

At the end of his performance, I ask, "How was the time in the bridge?"

"It fell apart," says Trevor.

"Why? Where was the concentration of the time?"

"In his foot."

And what happened? Did the foot get tired and the time fall apart? Please bring time into your core and then send it into various parts of your body. If the left foot gets tired, give it to the right foot.

Next up is Phil, a tall, outgoing twenty-six-year-old from a Boston suburb. A worried look is fixed on his face, and when he gets onstage and sings an a cappella piece, he complains about not having a guitar to accompany him.

I explain, "Phil, I sympathize with your situation, but what can I do? I won't let anyone accompany themselves yet. I know you usually have your guitar and that it helps you keep time, but I am trying to get that time to move inside you. I'm sorry about the hand you were dealt."

Let me tell you about the hand that was dealt to me one weekend recently. On Friday night, I played at Regis College, in Weston, Massachusetts, a suburb of Boston. On Saturday, I flew to Washington, DC, for two shows in a small club. I went to bed at two thirty in the morning and woke up at five thirty to fly home to Boston. Sunday morning, I attended a memorial service for my grandmother. That evening, in Concord, Massachusetts, I performed at a free outdoor concert with various other artists. By the time I hit that stage, I was fried. My brain was molasses. I knew that it was going to be a struggle to see or hear my audience clearly. However, I refused to compound my difficulties by beating myself up for not being one hundred percent. My responsibility was to monitor myself, take stock of what I had left, and do my best.

In my mind, I didn't play very well that night. I wasn't spontaneous. The cobwebs of fatigue didn't allow me to be nimble enough to respond to the moment. It was very frustrating.

People came up to me afterward and said, "Livingston, you were great!"

I looked them in the eye, shook their hands and said, "Thank you. I had a terrific time, too."

It was a bit of a lie. In truth, I didn't belong there. I belonged in bed or at least on a couch with a TV remote.

But what gives me the right to dispute or to take someone else's pleasure at anything other than face value? A compliment is a gift, and graciously receiving a gift is a very kind act. You do the monitoring. Let someone else do the judging.

Hecklers

If you're dealing with audiences in any kind of meaningful way, you're going to have to deal with hecklers. First off, let's define a heckler: I think it's somebody who is steadily and aggressively disruptive. They can be that way for three reasons: (1) they are angry, agitated and uncomfortable, and need to express it; (2) they are mentally unstable and unable to judge the disruptiveness of their state; or (3) the most usual, they are chemically blasted and oblivious to their reduced capacity for reasonable social intercourse.

If you're watching the space where you'll be playing before you go onstage, it's pretty easy to spot a group that will be disruptive—particularly if they're intoxicated. Be aware that the potential exists, but don't react too early. Let other audience members work on them first. Group pressure solves nine out of ten cases of boorish behavior.

If they turn out to be oblivious to group pressure, then eventually you've got to step in. After two or three concerned, serious looks in their direction, I tell them, "Guys, I'm not going to be here much longer. When I'm done, it'll be your turn."

I generally say that off mike and directly to them. Again, in most cases, that's enough to solve the problem. However, once in a great while—about once every two or three years—I'm faced with someone who is so disruptive that I have to speak with them directly.

I'll break rhythm, still my guitar strings and say on mike to the audience, "Excuse me for a moment."

I'll then either put down my guitar or not, depending on where they're located, and I'll walk over to the disruptive person. I go directly to them because we need to have a private discussion. What I'm going to say is so strong that I don't want any more of the audience than is necessary to hear it.

Be advised. It's definitely bad news to have the person who was onstage a moment ago walking in your direction with a deep frown on their face.

I crouch beside the person, make sure I have their attention, which isn't always easy, and say, "Your behavior is enormously disruptive, and I need it to stop. If it does not stop, I'm not going to continue to play. Do you understand?"

I stay with them until I'm convinced they understand, then I return to the stage. As yet, I have not ever had to leave a show prematurely (with the exception of the aforementioned "Tull Incident"). Be advised, these techniques assume a less than two hundred-ish capacity performance space. Beyond that, disruptions should be handled by club security.

Most audience troubles occur late at night. Many hours of drinking make for some interesting situations. A while back, I was playing a second show in a Chinese restaurant next to a tattoo parlor on Main Street in Woonsocket, Rhode Island (the location belies the long-standing commitment to great music that Chan's maintains).

I noticed before the show that there was a raucous table of eight or so people just to my right. Sure enough, when I started to play, they started acting up. The show was sold out, and I was under substantial pressure from the rest of the audience to stop this disruption. They, too, had paid their money and wanted to enjoy my show without the drunken intrusions.

"I wanna sing. I wanna sing something," one particularly blasted member of this group kept saying. I was inclined to let him try, but I had a problem. If I let him onstage and didn't control the situation, he might become a clown for his group—bringing them along and putting me fully out of control of the show. I kept cool until a plan occurred to me. I played a song called "On and On" by Stephen Bishop. During the bridge of the song, the melody goes up to a high A. Before I sang the line preceding the note, I looked over at the guy and said, "You want to sing something, don't you?"

"Yeah."

"Then come up here, right now, and sing this one note. Do you think you can handle that?"

Predictably, he stumbled up onstage, and I set the trap.

I sang, "Hold on tight / Don't let her say good night."

As the melody rose to that high A note, I left it for him. Nothing. He missed it completely. At that point, I turned to the audience and repeated the same line. At the appropriate moment, they seized the opportunity and sang the note clear, loud and strong. I instructed the would-be singer to sit down. He did and was not heard from again. Frankly, I was a bit lucky. My plans do not always work out so well.

Okay, it's time for performance.

Krystal sings a spiritual. She gets to the end of a fine performance, and a pained expression crosses her face.

I ask the class, "What about that last face?"

Krystal interjects, "I messed up."

Jason counters, "We don't know this song. Unless you tell us, we don't know that you've made a mistake."

Even if we did know the song, we don't mind a mistake. We're all human, and humans make mistakes. We forgive you: no harm, no foul. But, if you don't forgive yourself, if a small mistake is occasion for a pained expression, how is the audience supposed to feel? It tells them that you beat up on yourself for small things. If you can't forgive yourself for a small human mistake, how will you treat a very human audience? It makes them wonder and perhaps worry. "If she beats up on herself, yikes, what's she going to do to me?" Once again, self-acceptance and forgiveness are attractive qualities onstage. Sadly, they require a great deal of work.

Once, I was watching Phil Collins on TV, performing at the Live Aid concert that was broadcast all over the world. In the middle of one song, he hit a chord that was a complete miss. A slightly confused look crossed his face and melted almost instantly into a look of some bemusement as he then corrected the chord, smiled and played on. It was so very gracious.

Charlotte sings a Nanci Griffith song a cappella. Charlotte is from San Francisco. Attractively prim, she is firm in her belief that hard work and fairness will triumph. I hope she's right.

When she's finished, she asks, "During an earlier class, you said that when we're onstage, our job is to take in and make adjustments. Should we also try to build these spaces into our rehearsal times?"

"I don't think so, because you never know what's going to happen onstage until you're there," I answer.

What you want to do in rehearsal is to learn the content of your performance (songs, words, notes) well enough so when you are onstage, you can concentrate less on the content and more on what's happening around you. You can make your performance become part of the fabric of the moment. You rehearse so the performance becomes automatic and you are free to be completely neutral onstage, free to observe, process and react.

I ask the class, "Who has had a wonderful rehearsal only to have the performance turn into a nightmare?" All hands rise.

You play well in your room at night and then—kapow!—you're onstage being blindsided by events beyond your control. The playing field has changed.

Please remember: The rehearsal is no closer than a second cousin to the performance—a distant relation at best.

Ride, Dustin, Ride

"Dustin, do a little mental exercise for me. What street are we on?"

Dustin replies, "Boylston."

"I want you to imagine getting on a bicycle and starting to peddle down Boylston Street. Comfy?"

"Yeah."

"Cruising along?"

"Yeah!"

"Now you're approaching the intersection of Boylston and Arlington Streets. What are you going to do?"

"Uh, stop?" Dustin replies.

"What if the light is green?"

"Uh, go?"

"What you're telling me is you don't know what you're going to do at the intersection because you're not there yet. Right? Are you worried?"

"No."

"Of course not. You've ridden a bicycle for years, and when you get to the intersection, you'll make the appropriate decision. But it's impossible to plan in advance because you're not yet there."

Again, after forty-odd years and more than four thousand shows, the one thing I've learned for certain is that I have no ability to predict the course of a show until I get onstage. Everybody around me knows what is going to happen. Friends, managers and family will all have an opinion for me. They may have pieces of the picture, but how could they possibly know all of what is to happen. Show up neutral. Take in, then respond. Enjoy the process as it unfolds.

The Bat

The very best argument for performing with restraint, reserve and a neutral attitude is that it allows you to handle the unexpected. It has been my experience that when onstage, the unexpected will happen. It is the unexpected and unique events that are the source of the most vivid performance memories for both performer and audience.

A case in point: I was working the second show in Geddy's, a bar in Bar Harbor, Maine. The crowd was pumped, the joint was full, and the weather was uncharacteristically warm. The windows were open wide, and the touch of breeze felt great. Halfway through the show, a small—and doubtless very surprised—bat flew right through one of those windows. It was bedlam. Females with visions of having a rabid bat irrevocably tangled in their hair hit the floor with a scream. Males whose machismo was colliding head-on with memories of old cheap horror movies joined them. The bat, not at all understanding the sea of confusion that greeted his innocent search for bugs, zoomed around the room in circles.

As for me, I love bats. With the exception of a few humans and the occasional canine, it's maybe my favorite mammal—in this case, an innocent, industrious creature clearly involved with the wrong crowd. So, here's the scene: all these people were huddled on or near the floor, eyes glued to this circling, panicked creature. I concocted a plan. I instructed the people on the right side of the room to wave their hands and arms on my say-so. When the bat circled to the left, I gave the word. Their hands waved, and the bat's circle became smaller.

Progressively, toward the left, more and more people waved their hands and stood their ground. When finally confronted with no more room to circle, the bat took the remaining option and departed the way it had come. The resulting cheer was heartfelt and enthusiastic, and when the next song in the set was an abbreviated version of the *Batman* TV theme, a good laugh was had by all.

Next to perform is Dustin, a quiet, thoughtful young man with thick glasses that hide slightly sad eyes. He plays a challenging classical piece on his guitar.

"How did he do?"

Arnold says, "Well, he did very nicely, but he spent all his time watching his guitar. He didn't look around very much."

This is a dilemma. You want to stay in your instrument and concentrate on the nuances and subtleties of your performance. By the same token, you want to take in as much as possible of what is going on around you. If you cannot do two things at once, you need to prioritize. There is a solution.

Let's go back to Dustin. "Dustin, play a simple blues."

He begins to play.

"How is the rhythm? Is it better than before?"

Most say, "Yes."

"How about his eye contact with the audience? Does he seem as nervous?"

Kathy responds, "His eye contact is better. He's much more at ease—and really *cute*."

Dustin turned bright red, embarrassed by the observation, but in short, his second performance was far better than the first. He simplified things. He played a piece that was under his control. As a result, he had the time and space to check on his surroundings. He was more comfortable and more pleasant to be around.

If you carry music onstage with technical demands that monopolize your energy, you're asking for trouble. In the rehearsal hall, dorm room or next-door neighbor's garage, it all fits together so well. But throw in the complications of the onstage environment, and you have a recipe to crash and burn.

Instrumentalists seem to stay more within their instruments than singers do. Miles Davis comes to mind. However, think about Louis Armstrong or Kenny G. They always give the impression that they are plugged into the moment. They are aware of the audience around them. As a result, the audience feels they are able to communicate with the performer, to make a difference in the course of events—they are empowered and happy.

Jennifer performs "My Heart Belongs to Me." She does a fine job. She has great focus and stillness at the end of the song. We are transfixed. She's chosen a good song and performed it well. I suggest that hand movements and gestures would help to illustrate the lyrics. She balks.

"I never use my hands in normal conversation."

"Oh, really? Do me a favor. Help me with a skit."

I pretend to be a meter person writing out a fifty-dollar ticket when her car is parked in a completely legal space.

Jennifer gets into the swing of the skit and articulates justifiable outrage at the situation's unfairness. The class is amused to see her arms flailing wildly as she protests the injustice of the undeserved ticket.

You use your hands, arms and body in everyday life much more than you think. So when you *don't* use them onstage, it's unnatural and noticeable. The lesson here is to use your arms, use your hands, use everything you've got at your disposal to tell your story. If you don't have to hold an instrument, use that freedom to shape with your hands what is going on in the lyrics. No microphone keeping you in one place? Use the freedom to move around.

A good way to practice this is to speak the lyrics conversationally and see what gestures naturally arise.

In the early parts of your career, you may not have much external infrastructure (lights, sound systems, stages) to work with. Don't despair. This is the time to develop what's on the inside: a brain that can evenly and accurately process input from all the senses; cleanly disciplined rhythm to hypnotize the audience and allow your intimate observations to be safely shared; and the resiliency that allows you to take a licking and keep on ticking. Once you have the internals, you can entertain anywhere, with any externals that are around—or none at all.

CHAPTER FOUR

Reality

Whyen an audience comes to see your performance, they suspend their world and enter yours: the ticktock of your rhythm and the flow of pictures painted with lyrics, notes and chords on the jet black canvas of silence. That's the ideal. Let's get back to reality.

Here's a quiz for you: what's the difference between a preacher and an entertainer? Beep. Time's up.

A preacher gets paid on the *way out*. An entertainer gets paid on the way in. If you've taken the audience's money, you are an entertainer. You have been hired to pay attention to them. Do your job.

I ask the class about the clubs in which they have been able to play.

"The Jabberwocky Club at Syracuse."

"The Tam in Boston."

"The Knees in Worcester."

"How was the Knees?" I ask.

Laura says, "It was a scary rat hole."

"Whoa! That's pretty graphic. How was the sound?"

"Pretty crappy."

"The lights?"

"Almost nonexistent," she replies.

"Why didn't you ask for better?"

"I guess we didn't deserve it."

"No, no, no! I won't hear that. Of course, you deserve it. It's true, you're not going to get it, but you do deserve it. You are conscientious people, good sons and daughters, fine friends. You deserve the best.

But you're still not going to get it. Why?"

"The club owner is greedy and doesn't want to spend the money," she responds.

"Perhaps, but that's not why you can't get what you want. How good is your power base? At this point in your career, how many people can you draw into a club?"

Not many. Long faces indicate the class understands this reality.

The truth is, because you cannot yet draw a large audience, you cannot generate enough income to make demands of a club owner. So, you are going to have to make do with what is there.

I regularly work at a club called the Iron Horse Music Hall, in Northampton, Massachusetts. One time, I arrived at the club around four o'clock for a five o'clock sound check. When I went downstairs to go to the bathroom, I found it was pretty funky. So, I cleaned it.

"Ugh! Harsh!" says Kathy.

No, it was fine. I took some paper towels and used them to scrub down the fixtures. If I find trash and cigarette butts around a club's entrance, if time allows, I clean that up too (then I scrub myself down).

If an audience arrives and finds the outside or inside of a club to be dirty, chances are they won't readily return. But it is often overlooked by the owners. I wish the club staff would do these things, but they sometimes don't. Maybe they are too busy or they just don't see it (like the mess in my music room). For whatever reason, it isn't a priority. If I beat on the staff about cleaning the club, they are just going to get resentful, and any improvement in appearance would be canceled by the mutinous mood of already overworked staff having to perform extra duty. The ability to show up early and do the low and funky jobs speaks volumes about how seriously you take your audience.

I don't clean bathrooms and pick up cigarette butts for the club owners. I do it for my audience. They buy the tickets, and I work for them. In buying a ticket, they have hired me. They are my boss, and I don't like my boss having to stand in line looking at cigarette butts or using dirty bathrooms. Do they know I've done these things? I hope not.

When I am working in a club, I expect that place to come up to my standards. I don't care to go down to its standards, and I certainly don't want that for my audience. Detail, detail, detail. Good careers are in the details.

You're Not Paranoid—They *Are* Watching You

Your show starts not when you go onstage, but the moment you show up at the job. People are watching you: door people, waiters, bartenders and sound people.

How do you look when you show up for an engagement? Are you clean? Is your van beat up? Are you beat up? Is your equipment all dirty and taped? Are your electronics filled with buzzes? You're sending encyclopedias of nonverbal signals about the type of person you are. By your actions, you show other people how you want them to behave.

If you make a bad impression on the club's staff, then they can make your show uncomfortable in the extreme. Arrive early. Be nice. Look and listen. Identify and, if you're very lucky, solve problems.

Opening Act

When I am the opening act for an artist who is billed above me, I like to keep in mind that, in the main, the audience is there to hear the lead act. I direct my attention to making the headliner look good.

"Good evening. It is wonderful to be in Columbus tonight and to be sharing a stage with Bonnie Raitt. She is so fantastic. I'm going to play about twenty minutes, and then I'm going to turn you over to her."

If you are the opening act, *be quick* and *be good*. The better the opening act, the better it is for the headliner.

When I am the lead act, I love it when my opener is great because it reflects well on me. Sometimes I'll be sitting backstage listening to an audience go wild for the opening act. What's tough for my ego is good for my audience. If the opening act is terrific, be sure to acknowledge their quality so you validate your audience. And if you can work it out, get them to come onstage during your set. They're great, and you get the credit.

Keep in mind the same audience that thanks you for a good opening act will blame you for a bad one. It's grim to follow a terrible opening act. You step onstage, and the audience's gaze tells you, "Ouch, that hurt. Why did you subject me to that?" A rotten opening act can test the good humor of the best crowds.

When you're the opening act, even if you're doing very well, do not let the audience's enthusiasm keep you onstage too long. There's no better way to put yourself on the headliner's dirt list than to use up the enthusiasm of their crowd. *Know when to get off.* Be mindful of playing too long. The audience gets tired, the show runs late, and the headliner feels you've taken advantage of them. You won't be invited back.

If you're the opening act, make it your business to meet and discuss show length with the headliner. You'll find a remarkable disparity between how long the headliner wants you to play—six minutes—and the length of time the promoter or club owner wants you to play—two and a half hours. Find a compromise in advance.

I've had lots of interesting experiences with opening acts. One time, I was working at a small theater in Sarasota, Florida. The front doors were made of thick glass that was all smudgy. I arrived early and had some time to kill, so I got some Windex and began cleaning the doors. (It's amazing how this skill vanishes the moment I get home.)

Enjoying the simple monotony of the task, I looked down the street and noticed a young woman with a guitar walking toward the theater. An entourage of three followed her, and all four of them, shoulders squared, were obviously filled with the hopeful career implications of being the opening act for Livingston Taylor.

As they came up the steps, I held the door for them. Staring straight ahead, they purposefully walked right past me. They said nothing to me, violating our rule of speaking to everyone at the theater. The reason they didn't recognize me was simple. Their fantasy of a headliner did not include a window washer. Could that be Livingston Taylor with Windex two hours before the show? Impossible. Trust me, it's possible.

How Good Can You Be?

I ask the class, "How important is it to be good onstage? How important to play at the absolute top of your ability?"

As a unified voice, they respond, "Very important. It's the most important thing!"

What if I were to tell you that the audience basically doesn't care? Let's make up an example. Say you go to see Fleetwood Mac with a woman you've been seeing for about a year. You're crazy about her, and your relationship has been growing closer and stronger. You want to move it to the next level. So, while Stevie Nicks sings "Landslide," you lean close and whisper in your date's ear, "Sandy, I've loved our time together. I believe you are the most special person I have ever met. Will you marry me?"

With tears in her eyes, she kisses you softly and answers, "Yes."

Okay, how do you feel about the show? Yeah, pretty good. Did it matter that Stevie Nicks's voice might have been scratchy that night or that your seats weren't so great? That the sound had too much bass or the backup singer had a cold sore? No, of course not. In your memory, the concert is one of the high points of your life, and that song will forever be positively imprinted on both of you.

Now, suppose there's a couple at this same show for whom things have not been going so well. During this same song, she turns to him and says, "Tom, I'm sorry, but this isn't working. I've tried, but I can't get it back. We've moved in different directions, and I'm sorry to say there's nothing left. I'm all through. Tomorrow, I'm going to pack my things and move out."

How was the Fleetwood Mac concert for these two? Yeah, the worst. Forever in their memories, "Landslide" will remind them of one of the most painful moments in their lives—regardless of how well the band played that night.

I ask the class, "What big shows have you been to recently?"

Jason says, "Billy Joel."

"Where?"

"At TD Garden."

"Whom did you go with?"

"Three friends."

"Did you go to dinner before the show?"

"Yeah."

"How far in advance did you make these plans?"

"About a month."

You built an entire evening around Billy Joel. But his concert was just one part of your evening—albeit a crucial part—but hardly the whole night. So, even if Billy Joel's voice was a little scratchy, or his piano a bit out of tune, it was okay; *you* still had a great time.

I remember playing at the Old Town School of Folk Music in Chicago one night when my voice was virtually nonexistent, the result of a cold. I wasn't feeling particularly poorly, but I could just barely sing. But it was a sold-out house, and I had traveled a long way, so I went out on stage and sang half of one song. Then I said, "As you can hear, my voice is not what I would like this evening. But it's the only part of me that isn't delighted to be with you. So, here's what I propose. I'll leave the stage for a few minutes, and any of you who would like to leave and get your money back can do so without fear of embarrassment."

I left the stage, and when I returned, there had been virtually no reduction in the size of the crowd. I suppose they wanted to see just what it was I was planning to do to entertain them. I wasn't quite sure myself, but I started to play one of my better-known songs and to sing it very softly. Then I heard them, the audience, coming up underneath me to sing the melody. They knew I needed help, and they were there for me. It went on for the entire performance. After the show, members of the audience told me that they had a great time.

No one's asking you to be perfect. No one's asking you to be one hundred percent. But you are being asked to do the best you can with what you've got at the time. Does the audience care if you're tired or ill? Basically, no, they don't. They want to hear that you're glad to be in their presence, that they are the center of your attention. They will worry about you, if you ask them to, but they would much prefer that you worry about them.

Favorite Place to Play

"Livingston, where's your favorite place to play?" Arnold asks.

"That's a terrific question, Arnold, and the answer is simple. My favorite place to play is *always* right where I'm playing."

I often get this very same question from an audience member, and I am careful to be very place specific.

"Where's your favorite place to play?"

I look them clean in the eye, smile and say, "Right here in Steubenville, Ohio. *This* is my favorite place to play in the whole wide world."

They often frown as they search my face, looking for any hint of insincerity. They won't find it because I have told the truth. Regardless, they don't look long because they would love to believe that where I am is where I want to be. Actually, they don't really want to know my favorite place. What they do want to know is where they rank on my list. They're hoping for a high ranking. When they find out they're number one, they're delighted. I work very hard to put myself in a frame of mind that allows me to believe that wherever I am is the place I most want to be.

Play live any chance you get. Only by playing in front of people and watching them do you gain the experience and knowledge about the parts of you that work well with a crowd. There is a place, I think, at the beginning of a career, where playing for free makes some sense, but I wouldn't make a habit of it. An open mike night in a strong venue can give you experience in front of an audience and may catch the attention of the booking person for that room, but playing only for free will lead nowhere. Even the smallest amount of money will remind you that your music has value in the marketplace. When I first started out, my pay some nights was ten or fifteen dollars. Short pay, even in the age of dinosaurs.

Tim asks if my "favorite place to play" includes benefits.

In all honesty, I'm not crazy about doing benefits. Let me explain why and what my solution to the problem has been. The risks are high. The benefit really needs you to make money for them, and they expect your name to do the work. In reality, it is their organization that has to turn out to organize, promote and sell tickets. Their members also need to buy tickets. If the artist isn't famous enough to guarantee a good turnout and the show doesn't draw well, it will most likely be left on the doorstep of the artist. Not only does the performer not get paid, but they also get blamed for the failure of the event, and they have used up their playability in that area; they can't expect a paying gig there for six months to a year. So, often as not, everybody winds up a bit disappointed.

My solution to this dilemma has been to do *fundraisers* instead of *benefits*. I ask that the organization raise—either privately or corporately—the monies to pay my fee. This lowers their expenses substantially, and most of the money they generate through the event goes directly to the cause. If they can't raise enough money for my fee, chances are the show won't be a success because I am not enough of a draw. It may not be the best news, but no one gets hurt. If it's a cause I truly believe in, I can always take out my checkbook and make a donation.

Although more and more celebrities are doing political events, I try to keep my career apolitical. Politics is, by its very nature, a polarizing field, and no matter which side you come down on, you will alienate someone. I vote, but I try to keep my politics and my career separate. That said, I've found the pressures to do benefits and political fundraisers almost impossible to resist and wind up doing more of them than I think I should. I wish you better luck.

Lighting

In the performance classroom at Berklee, we have a small stage, a modest sound system, and a few lights. Laura stands on the stage and prepares to sing. Before she starts, we talk about lights. Good well-focused lights in the hands of a competent lighting designer are an amazing asset to a show. Bad lighting can be deadly. The lights we're going to get in the clubs we start out in are likely not going to be good. When in doubt, keep lights as bright as they will go and use plenty of clear, amber or pink gels; don't wash yourself out with greens, blues or purples—in the darkness of a club, you will simply disappear.

Bright white lights allow you to be seen.

Lee asks, "But when you have bright lights in your eyes, doesn't that limit how much you can see and how much contact you can have with your audience?"

Yes, it restricts your eye contact. However, bright lights do light up a portion of the audience as well, and you've still got your other senses to call on. If the audience can't see you, you are a voice in darkness.

My lighting rules are straightforward: Always use whatever stage lights you can. Keep them clear and bright. It is important to be more brightly lit than your audience so that you are the focus of their attention.

Once, during a career lull in the mid-seventies, I was hired to play at a small college in western Massachusetts. In the room where they were having the concert, there were no lights at all. It was basically a dining hall with poor lighting. I asked the student who was running the show if he had any thoughts about this oversight. He didn't. Because I had arrived early, and there was a Kmart nearby that I had passed on my way in, we had time to run over to Kmart and buy three clip-on-type floodlights, three hundred-watt bulbs to go in them, and an extension cord. We clipped them on the ceiling, where the acoustic tile met the metal frame, and the problem was minimally solved. With the room lighting turned off, my "stage" was the most brightly lit area in the room.

Occasionally, I am asked to play or speak spontaneously at a gathering where there is no lighting or sound reinforcement. My strategy goes something like this. First, I find the brightest spot in the room and claim it as my "stage." Then I begin, with my eyes, to find the exits from that room and to seal them mentally so that I don't lose people. Finally, I direct my attention to the most distant parts of the room and to the people there, gradually working my way forward to those just in front of me. I don't want to risk losing the people in the back by being preoccupied with those closest to me. So in my mental picture, I have cast my net over everyone in the room, and I proceed to draw them in.

Jennifer sings a pleasant ballad a cappella. There are periods during her song when she marks time and waits for another lyric to begin. During these times, she looks down at her feet.

I say, "Jennifer, how are your feet doing? Are they enjoying themselves?"

You might think about taking a moment when you are not concentrating on your singing to look around and see what effect your music and presence are having on the people in your environment. Look, listen, feel and think. Remember, on stage your job is to take in the reality that already exists.

Kathy gets onstage and sings Patsy Cline's version of "Crazy."

At the end, I ask, "How was that?"

Someone remarks that the time was a little shaky.

"Was she late in the time or did she rush?"

Phil says, "She rushed."

Think about that song. "I'm crazy (two, three, four) . . . crazy for feeling so lonely (three, four, five, six, seven, eight) . . . crazy . . . ." That's a lot of space when you're singing a cappella. With all that open space, I think Kathy got worried.

So I ask her, "Kathy, did you ask yourself if you should be doing something? Were you wondering if they would hang with you while you were waiting for the next lyric?"

"I panicked," she says, "and rushed."

Nothing tells an audience you are ill at ease like rushing the beat. It says, "Get me to the next phrase and get me out of here." Please avoid indicating to your audience that you are uncomfortable in their presence. Wait for the moment in time that is the beat with grace and dignity.

Sometimes the audience wants you to rush. A worked-up crowd in a bar is often guilty of this. In their passion to get higher, they will demand that the band rush. You must resist the temptation to fall into their euphoria. You are the "designated driver." Make them wait for the moment in time that is the beat. They will ultimately appreciate your discipline.

Please remember: An audience will never accept your passion unless they are held by your discipline. Passion without discipline is yucky.

Lee comes onstage and plays a simple piece with drumsticks on a chair. The playing is good. Yet when he introduces himself, I can't hear his name. I ask him to repeat it. He swallows it again. This is not good. People *must* hear your name. Tell it to them clearly, and maybe more than once. Make sure people know who you are. If someone doesn't know who you are, how will they ever find you? The more difficult the name, the more care must be taken in its pronunciation.

Lee looks down and is clearly worried about being onstage.

"Lee, you need to remember that when you're onstage, you are not running a democracy. You're in charge, and people want you to be. Accept the fact that you're not going to please everyone. Heck, some nights you're not going to please anyone. You have the right to do your show as you see fit. By the same token, they have the right to dislike it."

Jason asks, "What about instrumentalists? Miles Davis never responded to his audience in any way."

I find myself a bit reflective about Jason's accurate observation. You don't have to do any of the things that I talk about here. If you are an exceptional singer, instrumentalist or songwriter, you can be rude and abusive, and maybe, because you are so unique, people will withstand the abuse to get close to your genius. But how wonderful is it to be great *and* accessible—like Louis Armstrong, Paul McCartney or Bonnie Raitt. To share your genius in a caring, humane package is the best.

Since I give no tests or final exams in my class, I try to come up with questions to tease out their thoughts.

What is the difference between a good musician and a great musician? Between a good actor and a great actor? Between the good performance and the great performance?

I won't leave you guessing. The difference is: When you're good, you know what to do. When you're *great*, you know what *not* to do.

CHAPTER FIVE

Great Expectations

There is a serious lack of clarity about whether the major labels can or will continue in their traditional role as the vehicles for success in the music business. The onset of new technology and the subsequent market openings in which artists can produce and sell their own work has left the majors in the dust. As of this writing, the major labels are scrambling to maintain some portion of the control they have had since the beginnings of the record business, and frankly, they're in danger of extinction. If they are to survive, they will need to clarify and refine what it is they do for artists and audiences, rather than rely on what is good for the corporation. Although often reviled, they will, I believe, have a place in the future of the industry if they can evolve their roles.

Though major labels maintain control of the market for many of the older and more established artists, the new, younger generation has free rein to create and effectively market its own music without a label using home-studio software and the Internet. Record stores disappeared like morning dew as the music-buying population moved to cyberspace. It is a very exciting time, giving many more artists access to rapidly developing markets that unwieldy corporate models of distribution cannot reach.

For many reasons, I believe that major artists will continue to maintain corporate relationships in spite of the current upheaval in the industry. First, the corporation is desirable as the bridge between artist and marketplace. In order to sell millions of any product, we must reach beyond the several hundred people whom we can know on a personal level. The corporation provides publicity and marketing to those millions, allowing the artist to become a public persona (while maintaining a personal life not open to the public, ideally).

Secondly, the corporation has some financing (though presently less than in the olden days) to offer an artist to create art in a larger format. So instead of you and the band burning a CD in your garage, you now may have access to a real studio, a producer, an engineer and some great musicians to play with you. They can enable you to make better art. We will speak more about this financing and where it really comes from later on, but for now, the company takes the risk.

Thirdly, the corporation is equipped with a staff of legal advisors who can defend and protect your work, as well as perhaps establish a connection to publishers who may send your music on to other artists, jingle houses or film companies. Not many individual artists have this kind of access without a corporate alliance.

There is often a sense that the corporate world can elevate the artist to unimaginable heights from the smallness of the early career. Though this has been the case on rare occasion in the past, it is less likely as we move forward. The most successful partnerships are mutually beneficial. The corporation benefits from your art and audience, and you benefit in turn from its ability to grow and expose that.

So in the event you bump up against one of these huge entities, here are some thoughts on how to proceed.

I would ask you to think about the changes that have occurred in the financial structure of the music industry. Instead of taking in fifteen dollars or so from the sale of a CD, most of which is pure profit to the company, the corporations are being forced to sell individual tracks at ninety-nine cents per download, some of which they are losing to the online retailer, and they are losing business to file sharing, so their budgets are very limited.

If you want to play in the corporate pool, you will have to present yourself in a way that sells the company on how valuable you are. To paraphrase a well-known leader, it's not about what they can do for you, it's about what you can do for them. You have to trade in what I call the "currency of favor." Money is one form of currency, but favor is another. By favor, I mean energy, a shoulder to the wheel, or an ear that listens, as you fill the role of dependable friend or a gracious competitor. Favor has value and can be traded.

Let me give you an example. I got a call the other day from a young agent at a major booking agency. He was calling to ask me if he could add a young up-and-coming singer to the bill of my already sold-out show. I get asked this question a lot and often will agree, as I enjoy giving young artists a showcase in front of a crowd. My audience has been extremely kind about this, as a rule. But this was a major corporate entity, and I was wondering what the young singer would add to my show—what value he would bring to my audience and the venue. I posed this question to the agent, who admitted he hadn't thought about that. When he couldn't come up with any "currency of favor" for his artist, I asked him what he himself might do for me in exchange for the favor. Would he offer me an opening slot on a summer tour with a bigger artist, or even one night? No, apparently not. I apologized for my aggressive stance, and as the tension eased, I explained the "currency of favor" idea to him.

Once you are old enough to live outside the vertical hierarchy of your family and you move into life among your peers, you may find the "currency of favor" to be a useful concept. Be proud of what you have to offer, know what it's worth and let it be seen.

Now I'd like to spend a bit of time on a word that's used all the time in the entertainment industry and one you will perhaps hear more than any other in your career. That word is "no."

When a record company turns down your request for a contract, they say, "No." Does it mean that you are a bad person? That you don't have any talent? That your shoes are on backward? That your hair is too green? No. No just means "no." For that company, at that moment, you are not right.

How you accept somebody telling you "no" is going to make a big difference in your career. "No" is often painful. However, in the rinse of time, it can also emerge as a great kindness.

After being rejected by a record company, club owner or—most importantly—an audience, we may stay after them, making pests of ourselves, not wanting to believe they would turn us down. We may push.

"Why wouldn't you hire me to play in your club? I think my music is pretty good. How about letting me open up for somebody?"

Or instead of accepting an audience's indifference or even outright rejection of what we have to offer with grace and sadness, we start pushing. We hope that even though they didn't care for some of what we offered, if we push it all at them, they will miraculously change their opinion. It's not likely.

People have various ways of turning you down. The best way is with a simple, clear "no." But saying "no" is difficult for most of us. We hem and haw. We make excuses. We avoid the person. We duck and run, hoping they'll get the hint and go away.

If they resist, we often overreact and use anger to get the point across. The residual resentment is most destructive. The inability to hear and say "no" brings out the worst in everyone.

"No" is a wonderful thing to be able to say—quickly, clearly and without rancor. The best "no" I've ever received came from Clive Davis, a very fine record man and the former head of Arista Records. Because I admire his "ears" so much, it's always been an ambition of mine to record for him. To that end, I've sent him many demos over the years. The bad news is that in spite of my admiration for him, he never heard in my music what he needed to hear to commit his company to my career. The good news is that instead of leaving me hanging, the rejections were always clear and quick:

Dear Livingston:

Thank you for sending along your latest demo. Although it represents much fine work, I do not feel that any of the songs are particularly radio-friendly. As a result, it would be a most difficult project to market at this time.

Wishing you the best of luck in the future.

Clive Davis

Notice that he didn't say that he didn't like the work—or me. In his rejection, he is kind enough not to discourage me as an artist. As a result, my admiration for him continues, and I continued to send him my music.

While "no" is not always that gracious, it is essential to learn to recognize the many ways people have of saying "no" and then to accept their decisions. Your ability to hear and accept "no" will vastly increase the number of times you hear "yes."

Also, try to understand that it wasn't easy for the person who had to say "no." If you can do this, it says a lot about your character. Accepting the reality of a rejection allows you to move on, which leaves the door open for an eventual "yes."

This brings me to one of my favorite showbiz truths: "If you haven't heard, you've heard," and the answer is "no."

That said, it's very tough to know how hard to push or whether that one additional call may swing someone over, or whether a touch of well-timed begging will crack the door. What do I recommend? Certainly one follow-up call or letter is fine, but beyond that, be careful. Push, but avoid being obnoxious. Good luck.

Demo Recordings

Have any of you ever made a demo recording to get a record contract or club work? Sure, we all have. Demos are essential to the progress of our music. I like to view them as photographs—snapshots of my music at a particular place and time. Sometimes there are other musicians in my photo, sometimes not. Sometimes they're samples from a live show. Other times they're studio productions. Whatever you include in your demos, be careful about how much money you spend on them. Four or five songs seems like a good number to me. There will be time later for the other eight.

I've made demos for reasonable budgets and had them rejected, and then returned to the studio and quadrupled the budget expecting the quality to be four times better. It wasn't. Doubling a recording budget usually only improves the quality by five or ten percent. It has been my experience that with each doubling, the percentage of improvement gets smaller. It takes time to learn how to use a big studio budget. It's like giving a Maserati to a student driver.

Most importantly, avoid putting yourself in a financial bind when making a demo. If all you can afford is a single microphone in the middle of a rehearsal room, so be it. It's better than nothing and much better than being in debt.

I like to play my demos and watch people's reactions. Obviously, friends and family are going to tell you they like your music, but don't listen to them—watch them. Do they drift away as they listen? Also, watch for something else as you play your demos: how you feel. Are you comfortable or ill at ease? Are you pleased with what you've done or wondering if you can fit under the couch? Now, obviously this changes all the time, but patterns do develop. I make new demos all the time, and I include songs that worked well on earlier demos. I add them to the new mix—improving myself song by song, rather than reinventing myself each time.

A Changing World

I was in the dressing room of a dinner theater in Vermont, and they had a box of old records tucked away in the corner. A copy of Johnny Cash's *At Folsom Prison* caught my eye. It was a two-record set with twenty-two songs on it. It so happened that one of those songs was a monster hit for Johnny Cash called "A Boy Named Sue." Had you heard that song on the radio and wanted to own it in 1977, you had to buy the whole two-record set at eighteen-odd dollars. As you listened to all that additional music on your way to and from the familiar hit, a bond was created between you and Johnny Cash—and the revenue stream created by the purchase of the two-record set financed tour support and production values that reinforced the bond into a deep, lifelong commitment.

It's not for no reason that the geezer tours—Led Zeppelin, the Eagles, Fleetwood Mac, et al.—are the events doing huge numbers. Yes, the boomers have more money, but the relationship forged and tempered by prior record company commitment has outlasted the record companies themselves. I can presently order "A Boy Named

Sue" for ninety-nine cents, and the song will become one of 738 unconnected songs on my iPod.

My present thinking for my students is for them to envision their world and their careers with the traditional record-company model removed. If you are over forty, your view of a music career was formed with a backdrop of a massive record-company infrastructure. That infrastructure is now gone. Perhaps we should drift back to 1957 and see our careers in that context. Become a jack-of-all-trades: write, sing, dance, arrange, entertain and observe your audience. Use the Internet to promote your career and navigate it any way you can. The Internet will sort itself out, and new revenue streams will emerge. I'm convinced that it will be my students and their peers who will find the solutions. It is they who will discover a dependable revenue stream for "digitizable" creativity. Until then, stay alive and never doubt that your creativity is a precious miracle, regardless of its ability to make money.

Gatekeepers

The person responsible for the ultimate decision on the future of an artist is what I call a gatekeeper. There are gatekeepers in all of the arts: the gallery owners, the Broadway and Hollywood producers and, in the old days, the traditional record-label chieftains—Barry Gordy Jr. of Motown, Clive Davis of Arista, John H. Hammond of Columbia Records, and Ahmet Ertegün of Atlantic Records. These are often the people with whom we musicians had complicated relationships. If we weren't included in their sphere, we were resentful. If we were included and successful, we complained that they took too much money. (Never mind that the successful projects financed all the ones that never got off the ground).

The Web has removed much of the power base of these gatekeepers by taking control of distribution. Distribution was their source of revenue. Now, everyone has equal access to distribution, either from their individual websites or from iTunes, Napster, Rhapsody and the other means of downloading music. The question arises as to whether this has improved the quality of music. An informal poll of my students reveals that over fifty percent of the music they have downloaded was recorded before they were born; it's the music of the sixties, seventies and eighties—the era of the gatekeepers. Said simply, great art requires capital to concentrate talent and market the result. Presently, the Internet allows the unlimited distribution of digitized creativity for free. Until we find a way to pay for creative output, the world will remain unsettled and unpredictable. Nonetheless, now that "digitizable" creative sources (movies, books, music, etc.) have found their way to the Internet, a solution will be found. And I believe that it will be sooner rather than later. As I say in the title of a recent song, "Never Lose Hope."

The Web

I was driving along the Mississippi coast a year after Hurricane Katrina. It was twilight, and though the debris had been removed, nothing was rebuilt. The area was a forlorn and empty ruin, with one exception . . . someone had rebuilt the local Waffle House (a southern fast-food chain). It was bright, stark and new, and was buzzing with people getting food and companionship, enough to brave the daunting task of rebuilding the community. I think of that Waffle House when I envision our website. They are to be the islands of activity that promote ourselves and friends. The places people will go to remember that there's plenty of energy and creativity out there. I believe that it's through these websites that new distribution and profit streams will be found for digitized creativity in the Internet era that is upon us.

One of the skills I try to get across to my students is the ability to put themselves in someone else's shoes. This is useful in many parts of life, but especially in negotiations. So I want them to get to know, in their imaginations, the record company executives they may someday encounter. How do they feel? What motivates them? What's going through their minds? What are their fears? What are their needs? What problems do they have that you can solve? The same attention that we've learned to give to our audience can be expanded to include record companies and all the other people who are going to interface with our careers.

When we request and then agree to an alliance with a corporate structure, let's be clear what we're asking for. We're asking a corporate entity to connect our artistic endeavor with an audience that we may never personally know and that will never know us in any other way than the image the corporation projects for us. This is a huge and difficult transition point in our careers, going from the one-on-one, the personal interface, to a large base in order to market ourselves. It requires that we spend a lot of our time understanding and managing the maze of political and bureaucratic paths that exist in any large organization. This alliance is an essential part of our careers, but it is fraught with potential dangers, the greatest being that we may come to ignore our existing audience, the people whose initial support and loyalty made the corporate attention possible.

Statistically speaking, your early recordings have a small chance of being successful. If, in the heady spin of that recording process, you lose track of where you really are in the business and begin to believe the promotion filling the air around you, you can lose contact with your core audience. The people who loved you from day one. If you allow the bedrock of your success to erode, the corporate support will be withdrawn because you have lost your market. You're going to be in a lot of trouble. Never sacrifice a small but real fan base for a large, nonexistent fantasy.

It is not the beautiful and sophisticated that make our careers possible. In the early going, it is often the plain, the lonely and the overlooked that advocate for and support our art. Sometimes, an enthusiastic fan will ask me why I'm not more successful. I reply with a question: "Do you like me?" And the usual answer is, "Oh, yes." At which point, I like to smile and say, "I could never do better than that."

Contract Essentials

Starting out as a young artist, access to high-priced legal advice is often not an option. So here are a couple of thoughts to carry into negotiations with managers and labels. I believe a contract must have two things. The first is a performance clause, and the second is a time limit.

The Performance Clause

This is your voice, your melodies, your lyrics, your energy, your days and nights on the road. These are all tangible things that, when exchanged with an audience, can generate money.

I ask Krystal, "What does the standard management contract normally take as a percentage of the artist's gross income?"

Krystal takes a deep breath and replies, "Fifteen or twenty percent."

"Yes, and what does the standard management contract say the manager will do for the artist?"

Charlotte responds, "Help with the career."

"Jason?" I ask.

"Get the band work."

"Phil?"

"Do the business stuff."

Let's get the division of labor straight. The agent gets the work. The manager works with the agent to set the path for the career, chooses which record companies to approach, runs the money, advances the dates to make sure contractual issues are met, handles scheduling and press interviews, and acts as a general buffer between the artist and the industry. Management says no so the artist doesn't have to. That's what you'd expect a manager to do, but what the contract says is usually quite different. The common phrase used in management contracts is that "the manager will use his or her best efforts to further the career of the artist." Unlike the fifteen to twenty percent the manager garners, "best efforts" is virtually impossible to quantify. When you sign this contract, you have done something very common and very unfair. You have given away *something for nothing*.

I think this is important, so let me make up a bit of an example. Let's say a well-known management company likes you. They think you are great. They think you can become a big star. They want to sign you to an exclusive contract. You flip. Wow! Look at their roster—all the people whose names you see listed are very successful. They're huge! If you could have just one-tenth of one of those careers, you'd be set for life. So you sign with this company for an exclusive three-year deal with unending options. You agree to pay them twenty percent of your gross receipts. What does management agree to? "Best efforts." You are giving away twenty percent, and they are giving away "best efforts." If the relationship goes sour, drag "best efforts" into court and see what happens. Again, if you sign that contract, you are giving away something for nothing.

The conversation might go something like this: "I am so pleased that you think I have potential. What kind of money do you think I could expect to make in a couple of years? Really? That much? That would be wonderful. Why don't we put into our contract that if I don't gross that in two years, I have the right to end the contract?" It might allow the company to lower its sights to something more realistic.

Reward enthusiasm, but be sure to outline specific performance levels that both parties must achieve for the relationship to continue. Never give away something for nothing. From the business side, by the way, an artist overestimating his or her own worth is equally common and problematic.

For a record deal, the performance clause would be, in my ideal, tied to sales. If the label doesn't move a certain number of copies or downloads—whatever the current medium dictates—within the length of the contract, then the contract ends.

Termination Date

All contracts must have a termination date—that is, a date on which the contract is over, regardless of whether the terms of the contract have been met. Contracts written early in careers are notorious for containing clauses that automatically renew the contract when various terms of the contract are not met. Self-renewing contracts are like quicksand. The longer you stand there, the deeper you sink.

For a young career, the longest time a contract should last is three years. A longer commitment is unfair to the changing life realities of a young career. A shorter commitment can limit the return on investment required by a corporate structure.

So, again, here are my two suggestions for what should be in any contract:
1. a performance clause (Never give away something for nothing.)
2. a termination date (Never sign an open-ended contract.)

This advice seems so clear and easy, yet many people get bound by terrible contracts. I think this is because they are afraid. They panic, believing that if they don't take this deal, they will never get another chance. Their fear tells them there is only one star in the sky. This is not so. There are other relationships out there. Quality will be recognized, and it will shine. Don't give yourself away.

Take Me. I'm Yours . . . Sort Of

Arnold, ever mindful of the street side of life, asks me, "Livingston, do you ever worry about someone ripping off your songs when you send out demos?"

No, and here's why. When I write a new song that I want to send out, I mark my demo with "All songs copyright . . . ," naming my publishing company as the publisher. If and when I record the song for a label, I send that information to ASCAP (or BMI, if that's where you want to be), and they protect the copyright. If this really is a concern, you can burn a CD, name your label, and register the songs with ASCAP or BMI. You might want to do that before you put the song online, as well. If you're looking for additional security, send a registered letter with a CD in it to yourself and hold that, unopened, in a safe place.

It's time to move on to the performance part of class.

Dustin plays a difficult classical guitar piece. His nervousness causes him to stumble, which makes him more nervous. The tension is excruciating.

"Dustin, can you do me a favor? Play something so simple that you could do it in your sleep."

He starts to play an easy blues, but it's still too complicated. I have him humor me by playing only one chord every four beats. With the simplicity of the assignment, his shoulders relax, and he looks across the class and smiles. The tension leaves. The joy returns.

Okay. Dustin is at ease and confident with this piece. He smiles, we smile. He feels good, we feel good.

Always try to play within your limits, *well* within your limits. Performers are terrified that if they don't show everything they've got immediately, the audience will think less of them. Don't let your insecurity force you to attempt to spear your audience and reel them in. It's much better to hypnotize them with rhythm and seduce them with discipline. I say this over and over because it is such an important part of performing. Do not go beyond your comfort level. Do not ask your music and talent to do more than they can. You could find yourself disappointed if your talent doesn't live up to your expectations. Said another way, your music is fine; it's your expectations that need some work. Remember the difference between *expectation and hope*.

Phil steps on stage with his guitar and plays a simple folk song. He makes a mistake, and his face takes on a pained expression. It's a small mistake, but the pain we see is huge. He is beating himself up for being imperfect. Beating yourself up for being human is an awfully tough way to go, and it can scare an audience because they're human, too.

So, if perfection doesn't make a successful career, what does? As I've thought about this point at various times, I realized I needed a definition of success before I could figure out what a successful career was. I looked for a common thread in the lives I admired. It didn't seem to be about money, power or fame. Success seemed to be about gratitude. The ability to recognize that your presence here on the planet at this time is a gift and nothing more need be expected or offered. Gratitude is success; success is gratitude. They are interchangeable. It's true not just in a career, but in life in general. Self-acceptance, forgiveness and gratitude are very attractive qualities on stage.

Trevor gets on stage with his guitar, fiddles with the sound, tunes a bit and then announces, "I guess that's good enough."

When he finishes the piece I take exception to the phrase "good enough."

"Trevor," I say, "that phrase tells your audience you're settling. It is another way of saying, 'Don't expect too much.'"

Trevor, mildly miffed, challenges me. "Okay, what would you do in the same situation?"

I walk to the stage, pick up his guitar and fiddle around a bit. I look out at the class, stand totally still and say one word, "Perfect."

Now, everybody knows that the guitar isn't perfect, that I'm not perfect and that the audience isn't perfect. So what do I mean by "perfect"? It is another way of saying that I believe nothing could be finer than this intersection we've come to, in sync and together with an audience. Perfect.

I like that word, and I ask Trevor to go along with me. "Fiddle with the guitar, look at us and then say, 'Perfect.'" He does. The class cheers.

CHAPTER SIX

Radio and TV (Broad-Based Media Exposure)

As the change in the major labels has become somewhat unpredictable, so too has the fate of radio. Radio was and still is an adjunct to the major label, playing songs from CDs that label artists release. Without a label (i.e., a corporate sponsor) there is very little if any chance of getting any airplay, and even with a label, access to public airwaves is difficult. Now that the labels are undergoing such radical change, radio is left hanging, seemingly playing more oldies than new music, and more unwilling to take a chance on a new artist.

BSP is the acronym I use for "Big Shot Potential," and Big Shot Potential is what you get from *broad-based media exposure*. Let me sketch it out. You know how your girlfriend's or boyfriend's parents think you're a bit of a bum? They're not exactly delighted that their kid is spending time with an unemployed singer-songwriter, particularly when there are all those potential lawyers and doctors out there. Then one day, the parents hear your music on the radio, see an article about you in a magazine or newspaper, or see you on TV and—kapow!—the world changes. Being included in public media has given you one of the pleasant rewards of show business: BSP—Big Shot Potential.

Kidding aside—radio, print media, Internet and television are essential to the expansion of an audience. It used to be that radio was king. A record company infrastructure would deliver to radio a steady stream of music choices, and out of the two hundred songs released per week, any given station would choose two or three. The small stations would take a chance on a new release, and if it developed a buzz, it would be passed up the chain until it was a major hit at the powerhouse stations in major markets—a predictable path that created a catalog of music that is still supporting what's left of big radio today. As the Internet has changed so many things, so it is true, too, for new music exposure. Even websites that aren't dedicated to music—like YouTube and Facebook—help expose people to an endless stream of music from every direction, only a small fraction of which is exciting and new. As Bruce Springsteen dryly noted, "Fifty-seven channels, and nothin' on." As I've said before, I believe we must find a way to charge a fee for the digitized creativity that passes through the Internet. All creative sources that can be digitized— radio, TV, books, movies, newspapers, etc.—have had their revenue streams disrupted by this reality. Great art tends to grow in the soil of concentrated capital and talent.

"BME = BSP"

Broad Media Exposure remains the key to Big Shot Potential. Media promotion must remain at the core of any discussion with any potential corporate partner. Although press coverage, word of mouth, etc., all help, nothing works like heavy radio play. Although the world is changing, traditional radio and TV remain very powerful promotional tools.

Hundreds of thousands of people are listening to a major radio station in an urban market at any given moment. To reach that many people by touring would require, literally, years on the road. When your music is played on the radio, it's a three-minute commercial for you. Imagine what Coca-Cola or Apple or Volkswagen pays for that same exposure, and you're getting it for free . . . uh, sort of.

Let's look at the difference between radio and television.

"What's your usual physical state when you're watching television?" I ask.

Arnold says, "Lying on the couch."

Do you watch TV when you're driving? Hammering nails? Flipping burgers? Jogging? Of course not. Watching television is a passive act. When you listen to the radio or your iPod, you can be passive, but you can also do any number of things. Drive, work, study, date, sunbathe, party, shower. So you are living your life and the music plays. The music becomes a *soundtrack for your life*.

Who gets transported to another time and place when they hear a certain song? Everybody. A girlfriend, a boyfriend, a summer past, a group of friends, a job. Different songs remind you of different places. Sometimes it's the TV that connects a place to a song, but I feel mainly it's the radio. I hear "Our House," by Crosby, Stills, Nash & Young, and it's 1970 and I'm on Martha's Vineyard, a shy, skinny kid getting up the nerve to kiss a young woman upon whom I have a heart-stopping crush.

Or I'm at a truck stop south of Macon, Georgia. It's two a.m., and I'm eating eggs and toast after a week on the road. I'm tired and drained and completely available to be beat up by a song. And, boy, does it ever happen. It's a song I've probably heard twenty times before with no reaction. But now I'm ready. Bonnie Raitt singing "I Can't Make You Love Me" comes and gets me. Bad speakers in a greasy spoon, and it still finds me and slaps me around. Thump! Pow! Why didn't it do that the other times I had heard it? Because I wasn't ready. But at that diner on that late night, when I was tired and lonely, it got to me, and I cried. I needed to cry, and the song let me. It was the greatest. I was wet clay waiting for an imprint. Psychologically buck naked and ready to be branded. And Bonnie got me because she and I happened to be together at the right place at the right time. I suspect it's happened to all of us many times with many songs.

In forty years of making records, playing shows and enjoying delicious doses of radio play, I've done my share of branding other people. I see them come to my shows to relive these moments, and I'm delighted to help them in the recapture. Occasionally, I'll watch an audience filing in for a concert and spot a person who is totally incongruous to my usual crowd, perhaps a tattooed biker sort. The guy sheepishly finds a seat, and I wonder why he's here to see me. And then I realize, I've branded him. My music got to him some late night in some vulnerable corner.

I was playing a song of mine called "There You Are Again" at the Towne Crier Cafe in Pawling, New York. A woman to my left was softly crying as I got to the last verse. I asked her if this song had made her cry, and—a little embarrassed—she answered yes. I said, "Don't worry. It makes me cry, too." Touching people with your music is the best.

This is a major component of the maturing career. We have become part of the soundtrack of people's lives. Our songs remind them of past worlds. And when they want to relive those worlds, they seek us out.

Branding people with your music is mainly the function of random chance. Your music happened to be playing when they were wet clay. They were ready for something to impress upon them, and you were it.

Heavy rotation—that is, being played many times a day in as many places as possible—increases the odds of your music finding a receptive home. Media exposure is the essential ingredient for lifting your career to the next level.

Please remember: In every discussion with a corporate partner, you must include the question, "How are we going to get media exposure?"

How do you get your music on the radio? The person who makes that decision at the radio station is the program director (sometimes called the music director). That said, let's talk about the normal hierarchy of a medium-size radio station. It includes (1) the owner, (2) general manager, (3) program director, (4) sales staff and (5) disc jockeys (on-air talent).

"How does a radio station make money?" I ask.

"Advertising," Krystal says.

Correct. Do you pay to listen to the radio? Of course not. You are a passive recipient. You do not normally participate in any way in the course of a radio program. Although they desperately need you to listen, you are only indirectly responsible for their income. Advertisers finance everything.

"And how does a radio station decide how much to charge for an ad?"

"Ratings?" Phil suggests.

You bet. There are companies that survey the listening habits of the population in a station's broadcast area. Rating points go up, money goes up. Ratings go down, money goes down. Pretty simple. If the ratings go down, and stay down, there will be changes made and someone will probably lose his job. The owner? I don't think so. The station manager? Maybe, but tough. Salespeople? Never fire people who work on commission. That only leaves program directors and deejays. And the only one that concerns us here is the program director.

Program directors are the ones who make the decision to play our music. And they get fired constantly. They are the radio equivalent of baseball managers or record company A&R (artists and repertoire) people. So, when you bring your music to program directors, again put yourself in their shoes. Give them reasons why they won't lose their job if they play your music and their ratings drop. Think about them in a meeting with their general manager justifying their playlist. "Why did you play this Livingston Taylor record?" "Uh, I like his music, and I think he's a nice guy." I don't think that's the answer an angry station manager wants to hear. You've got to show that your record has gotten a good response in other markets and that a local competing station has added the record and is doing well with it. Show them that you've done public service favors for the radio station and are *owed a payback*—currency of favor! These are the reasons why program directors add records. If you can't give them these kinds of reasons, they are *not* going to play your music, regardless of how they feel about you personally. They've got to be able to cover their heinie in a period of down ratings.

Program directors receive hundreds of requests each week to add records. And why not? Your record, being played nationwide, is literally millions of dollars in free advertising for you. Sadly, I am not the only one who knows how valuable a hit record is. The competition for the few available slots is fierce. So what? Let it be fierce. I love it when the program director tells me he is going to play just two of the two hundred records he received in the past week. My response? "Who's the other one?"

Build solid relationships with program directors. Hear their needs, solve their problems, and get yourself on the radio. Although they regularly lose their jobs, they tend to be hired by the radio station that just fired *their* program director, and a positive memory of you travels with them.

If somebody is playing your record, write them, call them, thank them. Put yourself at their disposal. They are giving you free advertising. A letter might keep your record in medium rotation rather than light rotation, and that one extra play might be what's necessary to imprint one extra person. And remember, once imprinted, they are yours for life. There is no unimportant radio play.

In the late seventies, I was promoting a song called "I Will Be in Love with You" and was scheduled to appear on several talk shows of the day, including Mike Douglas, Merv Griffin and Dinah Shore. I called my executive producer and main booster, Charlie Koppelman, and asked him, "Why am I doing these shows when none of my audience watches them?" He replied, "Probably not, but the mothers of the program directors of the radio stations we want to be on may be watching. Any leverage we can get will help."

When an audience is completely familiar with your music as a result of radio play and the subsequent purchase of a record, a wonderful thing happens. *They learn their part.* You play two chords at a performance, and they know what's coming. They are completely at ease. You know the song, they know the song. You are free to communicate back and forth in a mutually understood language, the language of your hit record. It's a familiar and relaxed communication, and it's big fun.

Now, getting a record on the radio in competition with the likes of Elton John or Coldplay or Beyoncé can seem like a daunting task, and indeed they have millions of dollars in assets at their disposal. But there is a higher truth than money. That truth is that a great record is impossible to keep down. A great pop record demands to be heard. It cannot be stopped. It will rise to the top. To again quote Charlie Koppelman: "To have a hit record, all you need is a great song and a tape recorder." And we all have equal opportunity to find the great song and record it. I believe there's a lot of democracy left in the Top 40.

One of the reasons I am such a bear about record promotion is that you work just as hard to make and record music that is heard by no one as you do to make music that's heard by every set of ears in the known universe. I make my music to be heard, and I want you to make yours that way, too. People worry about asking for too much. "I just want a sweet little career with a couple of people who love me"—as though their humility will mitigate the sadness of rejection. A fall from a small dream hurts just as much as a fall from a big one. It's okay to hope for it all. (Note the difference between hope and expectation). Somebody's got to have the number one record. If it can't be me, it should be you.

Moths to the Flickering Light

Now, on to TV. First, I don't think much of television in spite of the fact that I watch a fair amount of it. TV is an enormously powerful tool. Treat it carefully. On TV, display the merchandise, but don't give it away. By that I mean, don't play too much of your music. One or two songs.

Television can have an amazing effect on a career. If given in the right doses at the right times, it is *rocket fuel*. But be mindful, TV has its downsides. TV is career cocaine. The second hit never gets you as high as the first. Television is to your career what white sugar and caffeine are to your body—a quick hyper buzz, and it's rather addictive.

As a viewer, once you've surrendered to TV, it's difficult to duck out of the way of its image. This is why advertisers love it so much. When your image is on TV, it leaves no room for imagination. Television can only show the thinnest veneer of what you are. It is a cold medium, and as such, it can make an artist into a cardboard personality—always on, always happy, smiling and upbeat. Because of this, it's very easy to become overexposed and boring. Far superior is the even "brown rice" of radio. There is no substitute for it. Radio is the background music for people's lives, and the more your music is played, the greater the chance that it will become the theme for a part of their lives. That said, if you are a very successful artist, you cannot avoid doing television, and you will want to do it. So learn how. Practice TV. Go on small local shows and check yourself out.

There are a few things I have found helpful regarding TV:

1. If there is no makeup, be sure to wash and dry your face. An oily look is most unattractive on television.
2. Avoid caffeine. The combination of adrenaline and caffeine will make it virtually impossible to play a coherent chord or sing an accurate note.
3. Begin counting the rhythm of the song long before you are introduced. Fifteen to twenty seconds is not too much. If you wait to start your count until the red camera light comes on, the rhythm is sure to suffer.

We are living in a time when everything is being recorded. Digital storage capacities are such that there is an electronic trail for all we do. Be mindful . . . clearly Big Brother is watching.

Don't Wet the Bed

Radio and television will not be enough. No matter how much mainstream media exposure you garner, live performance will remain the bedrock of your career. Sadly, there are fewer and fewer places to play live music. Equally sad, some of the musicians who play in the dwindling supply of clubs often behave like groups they have read about in *Rolling Stone* and *Spin*: they are abusive and self-destructive. These magazines talk about this side of life because stories of drunkenness, destruction and cruelty sell far more magazines than stories of normal, shoulder-to-the-wheel, clear-eyed work. But when a young group behaves poorly in a club by trashing the place— leaving behind a large mess and a small profit—the club owners may understandably give up and stop having live music. Listen, nobody knows better than me that small-time club owners can be unpleasant, but they do not deserve to have their establishments trashed. Bring the funky club up to your level. Don't descend to theirs. And *please remember*: That funky club may well be the last barrier between you and total obscurity.

Now let's play.

Jason sings and plays "Better Together" by Jack Johnson. It is a good well-known song. Although he is quite nervous, the quality of the song helps his performance. Because it is familiar to the class, it helps us understand where Jason is trying to go. A familiar song, or "standard," is a good translator for your audience. When they hear your version of a song they know, it helps them understand the new material you introduce, the songs they haven't heard before.

This concept was brought home to me one day at my local police station. I was there filling out a form for a pellet gun permit. (No, I'm not a Ted Nugent wannabe. A red squirrel had taken up residence in my house, and the resulting destruction had driven me to a homicidal froth.) While I was standing at the front desk with a police sergeant, a Scottish vacationer came through the door, and when he spoke, he was completely unintelligible to both the sergeant and me. He spoke again, and again we were baffled. Although he was speaking English, his accent was so thick that we couldn't comprehend him. After three go-rounds, with ever-rising frustration, he finally said a single word that we understood. That word was "direction." Click. Instantly, we understood all. The one clear word made the accent intelligible, and we were able to determine what he needed—which, by the way, were directions to Wayland, the next town over.

The occasional familiar song can be the translation key to a lot of new ideas.

Charlotte plays guitar and sings a Graham Nash song. She holds the rhythm in her picking hand. The inevitable happens. The hand gets tired, and the more tired it gets, the more tension and pain there is. I have her internalize the rhythm and strum just the chords necessary to support the melody. The song immediately becomes settled and focused.

Again, the rhythm must be within the core of your person. It must be internalized. The music hangs on the rhythm like clothes on the body.

Boris sings while Jennifer plays the piano. I have Jennifer simplify the part she plays by two-thirds, and predictably, the panic diminishes, and the focus increases. Does anyone think less of Jennifer's playing now that she is playing less? No, we like it more. So, if people sound far better playing less, why do they always try to play more? *Fear.* The insecurity says, "I must play it all right now. If I don't, I won't get another chance. I won't be heard, and I will disappear." The fear starts running the performance. So how do you quell the fear and stay within yourself? It's different for each of us. I personally use prayer and spirituality for self-acceptance. An ongoing conversation with a deity of your choosing might not help, but it can't hurt. I love the quotation attributed to the great physicist Niels Bohr when quizzed by an incredulous colleague about a horseshoe he had put over his door for good luck. "You don't believe in those silly superstitions, do you?" the man asked. Bohr replied, "No. But I understand they work whether you believe in them or not."

Krystal sings. She has a beautiful voice, delivering a lovely song—but her arms are stiff, her hands frozen. I ask her to re-sing the song using her hands and arms to help illustrate what is happening in the lyric. "Overdramatize, Krystal. Overdo the hand gestures for now. We can tone them down later." On the re-sing, the class much appreciates the way the arms help focus the lyrics. And although Krystal remains insecure, it is a big improvement. Watch Jane Oliver, Barbra Streisand or Michael Bublé work their arms and hands into their songs. If you've got it, use it.

We set up some microphones and continue the day's performances. Laura steps up to the mike and yells, "Check, one, two, check."

"Laura, is that your performance?" I ask.

"No, I just wanted to make sure the mike was working."

"Instead of yelling 'check, one, two, three,' why not lightly sing 'check one, two, three'? It will give you a much better sense of how the system sounds. And if people are in the hall, it will make them laugh."

Kathy asks, "What if people are there? Should they be cleared out during the sound check?"

I generally think not. Let them watch the process. Acknowledge and include them. Make them feel that they are now insiders, because, as insiders, they will have a vested interest in your show going well. Also, it's less work to include them than to kick them out.

Charlotte sings a Joni Mitchell song. It's keyed a little high, and with a whole tone reduction, it's much improved. Pay close attention to the key as it relates to your voice and lyric. A little change can help a lot.

"Okay. Who brought that bucket? I want to hear that bucket next." A tall, gangly fellow steps up.

"Hi, I'm Tim, and I'm gonna play a bucket." Racket and bedlam ensue. When Tim's finished with his "bucket sonata," Phil and Kathy express confusion about the end of the performance. It's particularly important with the avant-garde or unfamiliar piece to first use stillness, then a bow, to define the end of the performance. It's unsettling for an audience not to know when to clap.

Remember, when you get through playing, the audience often doesn't know how you did. Their reality is still suspended, and they're looking to you for information. With a light smile and pleasant countenance, you nonverbally inform them that what they heard was good, and although it might have been strange and new, they can go ahead and like it.

With the aforementioned smile and hopefully pleasant countenance, I pass out teacher evaluation forms and leave the class. For my students, it's *payback time.*

LIVINGSTON TAYLOR

CHAPTER SEVEN

Doing What You Have to Do

"**L**ivingston, is that you singing the Little Debbie Snack Cakes commercial?" Lee asks at the beginning of class.

"Yes, it is Lee. Do you think it's a bad idea for me to sing commercials? Does it cheapen my voice? Does it mean that I've sold out?"

Lee replies, "I don't know, maybe a little."

I used to think it would be wonderful to make a living doing only the things I wanted to do. But I discovered a pleasant reality while doing the things I *had* to do. It's the things we have to do that take us to magical places. The early-morning flight to Newark, New Jersey, forces us to be up before sunrise and puts us in a position to witness the dawn of a new day.

I have a small airplane, and sometimes when I fly to a show the weather on departure will be terrible—not dangerous, mind you, just crummy. With skies full of rain and turbulence, I'll take off, and as I gain altitude, the rain diminishes, the clouds above me lighten and then all of a sudden, I break out into a crystal-clear world of sun and blue. I am the only person in an unseen world above the clouds. And it is *so cool*.

If I'd had my choice, I would never have rotated into that mean sky, and as a result, I would have missed the elation on the other side of the clouds. The things we have to do often lead us into unseen worlds filled with new things to become passionate about.

I try to be careful in judging other people's use of their talent to make a living.

Please remember: When you're starving to death, all food is health food.

Commercial work is a very different world from recording. First of all, it requires that you become a member of the Screen Actors Guild or the American Federation of Television and Radio Artists. These are unions—and powerful ones. I sang that commercial for Little Debbie because with a certain quantity of earnings through SAG or AFTRA, I would get my health insurance paid for. Also, singing and writing music is what I do, and if Little Debbie Snacks wanted my music, I would be more than happy to provide it for a fee.

I see myself not only as an artist, but also as a craftsperson. As long as it's not too corrosive or destructive, I'm glad to give it my best shot. Also, what I will or won't do very much depends on my situation at a given time.

A number of years ago, I was recording a CD called *Life Is Good*. I was paying the bills myself: musicians, studio time, producer and engineer. I was getting down to the bottom of my resources and needed twenty-five thousand dollars more to finish the project. I was just about to borrow the money by taking out a loan against my house when an ad agency called and asked me to sing a beer commercial. I explained to the agency that I didn't feel very good about using my music to promote beer sales and that I was probably going to pass. But before I did, I asked how much they were willing to pay for my services. The reply was music to my ears, twenty-five thousand dollars. I found it remarkably easy to sit on my morals, sing the commercial, and use the found money to finish my CD.

By the way, thanks to that found money, the CD came out, got some radio play, introduced me to a whole new group of people, and gave my career a terrific boost.

Soft Pillow, Hard Floor

As my students and I spend more time together, I confide in them this reality: the performing arts are tough fare. I look at my students and explain that they are *my competition*. I want them to feel free to come after me. It will break my heart to be replaced, to be knocked off my spot on the hill—but at the same time, I respect the tenacity required to get to the top.

"Make no mistake," I tell them, "I want you to be able to take my place, but I am not going to step aside and turn it over. You're going to have to earn your seat at the table."

Many times you'll find yourself in competition with others. Don't be surprised if the winning doesn't make you feel as good as the losing makes you feel bad. Performers are often shocked when success doesn't bring the expected satisfaction. Winning is bittersweet at best. You triumphed over friends and colleagues who were perhaps equally qualified.

The illusion of life at the top is just that—an illusion. There's no certain point in your career where the going gets easy. The details in the struggle change, but the struggle remains. When you're at the top of the game, your competition is often at the top of theirs, and it is as difficult to maintain your spot as anywhere on the climb. The acceptance of this reality will dictate how comfortable you will be with success and recognition.

I believe there are three gates through which you must pass on your way to recognition:

The first one's quite easy: are you good enough?

The second one gets harder: do you want it?

The third gate is the most difficult of all: are you tough enough to get it?

Are you tough enough to see and face your weaknesses and then commit the time and energy to lift the low points of who you are? We all hope that we're so good at what we do well that no one will bother with our weaknesses, but I don't think that's realistic. I believe that we are chains and are only as strong as our weakest link. The good news is that working on our weaknesses is enough. Honestly facing ourselves strengthens our weak links with humility, bringing welcomed light into the darkness of fear and insecurity.

Prayer

There comes a point in your career where all the conversation, rationalization, introspection, detachment and observation do not work. You're moments away from being face to face with your audience, and in spite of your best efforts, you're sick with fear and nervousness. There's only one place I've been able to turn for any relief at all. And that is to a conversation with a force beyond my comprehension. I turn to prayer. I use the term "God" because of the tradition in which I was raised, but if "God" doesn't fit your belief system, please find a substitute. There are many forms of spiritual entities and structures that take the responsibility out of your hands. I love that humans use deities as repositories of unknown truths, and that there is a force that we believe sees and knows all and that allows us to solicit divine favor. It allows us to sail forward into unchartered waters filled with hope that the unseen deities will view our enterprise with favor. I do love the higher powers.

It took me a long time to get back to praying after it failed me as a young boy. There were five of us children, and when I was eight, my parents took us all on a summer trip to Europe. At one point, the three older siblings and my parents went to Italy for two weeks and left my younger brother, Hugh, and me in a youth hostel in Switzerland. It was awful. The staff felt that my brother and I were little rich spoiled American kids (probably not an inaccurate observation), and they were determined to give us some good Teutonic discipline. Oh, how I hated that place. Each night, I prayed to God to have my parents return and rescue my brother and me, and each morning I was still there, my prayer unanswered. By the time my parents finally showed up, my relationship with God was toast. God was not there, not home—or if he was home, he was too distracted to be dependable.

However, human beings must be able to call on the universe in times of need, so as time went on, I cautiously tried getting in touch with God again, to find ways to make God a more dependable ally. When nervousness and fear threaten to drown me as I take my place before some important career event, I love having a conversation with God. But what I enjoy saying is thanks. I thank God for putting me in a position where I can be nervous. If I'm nervous, it's because it's important to me. I asked for it. I asked to be in this place. I wanted to be at bat, and now I am. I've been given what I asked for. Pitch the ball. I'm ready for whatever happens.

I'm not sure anyone knows what God responds to, but it has been my experience that God, like an audience, responds much better to gratitude than to complaints. And it's much easier for me to get good results when I don't get too specific, so try not to request the color of the new convertible. Also, I try to maintain an ongoing conversation with God. It's much harder to get a hold of somebody when you're in a panic if you don't have the phone number memorized. So a regular—and by that I mean daily—conversation with the power of my choosing is a bit like money in the bank to me. I put in those gratitude deposits, and then when the heat gets on, I know just where to go for a withdrawal.

I try to remember that God is driving the bus. I make the occasional direction suggestions if I must, but I try to enjoy the view. And I'm not surprised if the suggested turn doesn't happen. The universe is neither for me nor against me. Watch the universe instead of waiting for the universe to watch you. At the very least, you'll have more fun. I think that it is a good idea to have a place of stillness in your life where you can go when times are difficult, a sense of faith in something larger than the human entity, and a feeling that, as former Prime Minister of Canada Pierre Trudeau so aptly put it, "The universe is unfolding as it should."

Autographs

I grew up in Chapel Hill, North Carolina, where my father was dean of the University of North Carolina School of Medicine. One warm late September evening, I was walking across the campus. I was thirteen years old. There was a concert going on in Memorial Hall, and in those pre-air-conditioned days, all the windows were open, allowing this amazing music to spill into the soft night. Curious and nimble, I climbed in a backstage window and, keeping out of view, was able to look over the band as they played to the audience beyond. Fronting the band was a very old man. After the curtain closed, he almost collapsed. When the curtain opened again, like magic, he was full of life. The curtain closed again and again he seemed near to collapse. Again the curtain opened, again he had total energy! That an audience had such power fascinated me. Even at that early age, my report card suggested that I might poke around for a career alternative, and this audience magic thing showed promise.

At the end of the final curtain, the audience filtered out of the hall. After a time, the band leader with his trumpet left and began walking slowly toward his bus. I approached this tired old man and, filled with youthful presumption, asked for his autograph.

He stopped, looked at me and asked my name.

I said, "Livingston." And he wrote, in the most beautiful, clear handwriting, "Livingston, Best wishes, Louis Armstrong."

When someone asks me for an autograph, time permitting, I have a path I like to take. First, I ask their name. "Jane." Then I say, "Is that ...J-a-n-e?" I *never* guess at the spelling; I always double-check. If the name is misspelled, the value of the autograph is diminished. Then I write something like "Best wishes" or "Much love" or "Thanks for listening." I like to keep greetings simple and fairly conservative. When I sign my name, I make sure it's readable. When and if somebody shows my autograph to somebody else, I want that person to be able to read and understand the signature. One time, I got Muhammad Ali's autograph. It was illegible. This was completely understandable, as he was in the middle of a crush of people when he signed it. But when I show it to people, I have to tell them whose autograph it is; its effectiveness is smaller.

Lastly, I date the autograph; when someone comes back to see me years later, it's fun to see the date. People remember the moment, and the date keeps it clear when the moment was.

An autograph will not help your career in a big way. It's a small career thing that takes surprisingly little effort to do well. It allows you a moment to be gracious to someone who admires you, and if done well, it will wind up on someone's wall where it becomes a promotional vehicle for you for the foreseeable future. Everybody visiting that room and seeing the autograph will be regaled ad nauseam with the story of the encounter. I like to help my career in the big ways, but find I have much more opportunity to help it in the small ways.

Hit the Road, Jack

Let's talk about travel and equipment—that is, the physical act of being on the road and the machines and electronics we use while we're out there.

When you are starting out, you and your band are going to spend a lot of time playing with used equipment and driving around in beat-up old vans. Why? More than likely that's all you will be able to afford. Even so, there are things you can do to make the experience of using used equipment less eventful. Though these suggestions will require a bit of an investment, they may pay off "down the road."

Here are some suggestions if you're going to be driving that old van:

- Steam clean the engine and drivetrain. It is much easier to find and work on problems (and there *will* be problems) on clean equipment.
- Replace all hoses, fan belts and windshield wipers.
- Change all fluids (coolant, brake, transmission, rear differential, engine).
- Check the brakes and tires.
- Buy a new battery.
- Replace all burnt-out lightbulbs—not only for safety but also to avoid late-night encounters with bored police who love pulling over old vans that are obviously full of musicians. The burnt-out light gives them a reason to stop you.
- Keep gaffer's tape (also known as duct tape), wire, and a Swiss army knife on hand—they can solve a remarkable number of mechanical problems.
- Own long, high-quality jump cables.
- Don't forget your cell phone charger.

Here are some of my "rules of the road." I am sure to leave early so I give myself enough time for things to go wrong. I always travel as far as I can as soon as I can. Travel first, rest later. The exception to this is that I don't drive if I am exhausted. I pull over and sleep for an hour and then drive farther.

If I'm traveling by plane, I like to fly early in the day. The later it gets, the more delays are compounded. I try now to leave after the morning rush at security, so between nine and twelve noon seems to be the best time. If there's a mechanical delay and it's suggested that I deplane, I always take all my carry-on belongings with me. Waiting to get back on a plane to get carry-on bags limits my options to take another flight if it's available. I play the "I've got a show to do and people are depending on me" card. All is fair in love, war and canceled flights.

Also, I try not to use smaller airports. Getting stranded in out-of-the-way places offers few alternatives. I try to stick to big hubs. Nonstop flights are always preferable. The rule of connecting flights is: all will leave on time except your arriving flight, which will always be late. When I fly, I rent cars at my destination. It is an added expense, but I feel it's worth it to maintain my mobility and get a chance to familiarize myself with my environs, and it gives me an opportunity to rest after my travel before beginning my show. Waiting for college students or club owners to pick me up is an invitation to adventure at best, but more often, to disappointment. I carry a portable GPS everywhere. After thirty-five years of bad directions, a GPS is truly a miracle.

At baggage claim, I open my cases and check my instruments. If the neck of my guitar is broken, I'd rather know at the airport than when I arrive at the venue. The earlier I discover a problem, the better the chance I have of solving it.

I change strings often and early. I don't fix broken guitar and microphone cords. Once broken and repaired, they will always work fine until the most critical part of a show. I throw them out and buy new ones.

Just a mention about wardrobe on the road: I like to change my clothes just before I go onstage. I have to be careful about what I pack because all the clothes I wear I also have to carry. The fresh clothes get saved for the show. The next day, I often wear the shirt I wore onstage the previous day, but sometimes, if I've played in a dive, it's too funky to put on. Then it's either search the laundry bag or break out a fresh one. I generally have pants that I play in and pants that I travel in. With any luck, you can get a couple of days' travel out of a pair of pants. A tip for changing your clothes when the dressing room floor is so funky you're worried that to step on it barefoot might result in unwanted pregnancy: stand on top of your shoes.

To carry my clothes, I've found a sturdy garment bag to be good and convenient. It hangs up easily in hotel and dressing rooms and is accessible when opened up. Do not overpack. If you need it, go out and buy it. It will still be useful when you get it back home. If I wash socks and underwear in the sink, I hang them over the lamps in the hotel to dry. Be careful. Trashing hotel rooms is one thing; burning them down is quite another. I recently surrendered to a wheeled garment bag. Yep, from now on, I'm "walking the dog."

In terms of finding food to eat, I have little advice. A club sandwich with potato chips is hard to mess up. But when it's two a.m. and the only place open is the 7-Eleven or the Toot & Scoot—kids, you're on your own. Frankly, I don't want to know. But I'd stay away from pickled eggs.

During the day's performances, Boris sings with a CD backup, and during the course of the song, the machine "breaks" (actually, I turn it off). Binding yourself to an inflexible computer program or CD guarantees that if there is a problem, the destruction of the performance will be total. Now, I've lip-synched my songs a number of times, the most memorable for me being two appearances on Dick Clark's *American Bandstand*. I love the freedom of lip-synching, just being cool in front of the camera, and not having to worry about lyrics or pitch, but you have to be sure to match the recording. Doing it live is high risk, but if your nerves can stand it, it's a great skill to have. Remember the first rule of "the technical": if something's going to break, it will always wait until you're most vulnerable.

Again, wherever you are going, arrive early to leave yourself time to solve problems. And when you travel, to paraphrase King Edward VIII, never pass up an opportunity to shower, rest or go to the bathroom.

CHAPTER EIGHT

Yahoo! Sex, Drugs, and Rock and Roll

Let's move to a discussion of two subjects that seem to preoccupy most everyone: sex and mood-altering substances.

Let's start with sex and the difficulties that arise when we attempt to use our sexuality beyond our own comfort zone.

"Has anyone in this class, male or female, ever been exposed to sexual harassment or unwanted sexual advances as a result of performing?"

Kathy responds, "Sometimes drunk guys try to come on to me when I'm playing in a bar."

"And Kathy, how does it make you feel to have some intoxicated guy come on to you?"

"Ugh. Nasty."

It's awful to be making your music and have people after you that you don't find attractive, people using your beautiful music in an attempt to exploit you sexually.

Our sexuality is one of the most important things in our lives. It's wonderful to look in the mirror and feel that you're an attractive person with much to offer. However, we all have different comfort levels in terms of how much sexuality we expose, and those levels change dramatically depending on the environment we're in. The real problem comes when we use inappropriate sexuality in an attempt to advance our careers. An unbuttoned shirt, too little clothing, a provocative pose, the use of sexuality to get attention—it's a Faustian bargain. We want so badly to be noticed. We want so badly for our music to be heard.

It's more likely that this behavior will put you out on a high sexual ledge. Standing on a high ledge is bound to leave you tense and ill at ease. Overt sexuality has never been a substitute for exacting rhythms and disciplined melody.

Please remember: It's a lot nicer to wish somebody found you attractive than to wish they didn't find you attractive.

Rusty, a former student of mine, went with his band to New York City where they were scheduled to perform in a gay club. When he and his bandmates arrived at the club and it was time to go on, the manager suggested the men take off their shirts. Rusty acquiesced but confessed to me that he felt cheapened and discouraged by appearing shirtless onstage. Some of his bandmates, however, thought it was fine to be shirtless. What to do? Don't make this type of decision at the spur of the moment. If you have not discussed it, take the conservative path.

Sometimes I'll pull off my vest if I get warm onstage, prompting the occasional hoot from the crowd. I like to look at them and say, "Remember my age. Trust me. This is as far as you want me to go."

Mick Jagger, Tom Jones, Beyoncé and Tina Turner are entertainers who use a large sexual component in their performance. Their apparent comfort with their sexuality is a source of both relief and amusement. They can turn it on and off because they are aware enough of what they're doing to know when the sexual innuendo is appropriate and when it's not. They are fully in control of this nerve-racking game. Their comfort in these areas is a result of years of experience.

Let's move on to booze and drugs. Imagine for a moment that you are going to consult a lawyer for the first time. You're welcomed into his office, and after the introduction, he nods, smiles and asks to be excused for a moment. He opens his desk, pulls out a can of beer, pops the top and chugs away. After a belch, he fires up a fat boy, inhales deeply, stifles a cough, exhales a cloud of smoke, and then, through glazed eyes and a purple haze, he asks about your legal problem. You wouldn't stay five seconds. This would be insane behavior from a lawyer, doctor or pilot. For a band on a gig, however, this does not seem that far out of line.

How is it that a bus driver drinking a beer on the job will immediately be fired, yet it barely elicits a second glance coming from a working musician? The arts are viewed as being rather undisciplined; wild and wonderful creativity can exist in some rather seedy and unfortunate places.

I'm reminded of a time early in my career when I was performing with a number of other acts at the Capitol Theatre in Port Chester, New York. After finishing my short set, I joined a few friends in the audience. The group following me was a southern boogie band with an Allman Brothers Band flavor. The front man for the group was attractive and well dressed. Unfortunately, he was also blasted. The extent of his excess became apparent to him only when he stepped up to the microphone and saw a large crowd all anxious and ready to be transported to some new place. Realizing his total inability to handle his responsibilities, he explained, "Hi, y'all. We were backstage gittin' ready and, uh, it looks like we mighta gotten a little *too* ready."

Frankly, I don't remember the outcome of his set, but I do vividly remember his total panic upon realizing that he had been called and was not ready.

Please remember: When you perform, you are responsible for the safe passage of your audience through your space.

You are the *designated driver*, the lookout, the early warning system. In spite of what they say, your audience does *not* want you to party with them. If they perceive that you are out of control, responsible people will remain on guard, diminishing the extent to which they'll immerse themselves in your reality. Making them feel secure will allow them the freedom to totally involve themselves in your performance. Above all else, the audience must be safe.

Jimmy Buffett is the ultimate designated driver. His manner is comfortable and relaxed and, at the same time, vigilant. Party your brains out. Jimmy's having a great time, but he's on the lookout, and if there's a problem, you'll be the first to know.

I was touring with Buffett in the early 1980s, and our travels took us to an outdoor show in Denver. Before Jimmy came onstage, members of the audience began throwing balled-up paper cups at one another. Jimmy, not liking the direction this diversion was taking, stepped onstage and admonished the crowd to "knock it off," at which point, somebody threw one of these balled-up cups directly at him. As his face darkened, the audience froze in fearful anticipation. Jimmy scolded them like children. "Don't you *ever* do that again," he chided with a pointed finger. The crowd, clearly sorry for their lack of control, wished for his forgiveness, and it was immediately forthcoming. The incident was forgotten, and the party-concert continued.

Headline News

Destructive behavior is far more fun to write and read about than good, responsible living. I personally love looking through the tabloids in the supermarket checkout line: "Cher Has Sex with Alien Bigfoot, Gives Birth to Drug-Addicted Siamese Green Peppers."

How much more exciting this is than an article on Livingston Taylor's average day: "Then Livingston took an early flight to Detroit, drove to Ann Arbor and checked into his hotel, where he went to sleep for the afternoon. Fully rested, he executed a clean, sharp show, had a very mediocre meal at Denny's, went to bed, and arose rested and ready to continue his tour." *Boring*.

Music publications often derive a large part of their advertising revenue from tobacco and alcohol companies. Chemically induced destructive behavior is sought-after copy in these youth-oriented publications. The fact that some artists have had career success in spite of their chemical problems makes it easy to believe that chemical saturation is no big deal. It is a big deal. Make no mistake about it, the long-term success of people who abuse drugs and alcohol is the exception. For every band that does okay in a chemical haze, there are hundreds that are self-deluded, out of control, fearful and blind, drifting into queasy mediocrity. Not my idea of great entertainment.

As for drugs, they are illegal. If you are caught with herb by an unfriendly police officer, you *will* enter the criminal justice system.

The criminal justice system will consume lots of your time and money. If you must take illegal drugs, be discreet. Don't take them in the company of other people, because when you stop taking them—and you *will* stop eventually—you'll very much regret people having seen you get high, and memories of the drug scene will be a source of embarrassment. Check out the baby boomer politicians trying to deal with past drug transgressions. In a focused career, there is little room for alcohol or drugs.

Fair Is Fair

At the end of every evening's performance comes the moment of "settling up." Clarity at this particular moment is never a bad thing. For example, I was working in a small club in Cleveland a few Decembers ago, and it snowed the night of my show. As a result, the crowd was quite small. The club owner had guaranteed me $4,000 and had paid me a deposit of $1,000. He still owed me $3,000. At the end of the evening, I went to his office to settle up. He had the $3,000 in cash for me. I asked how he did at the door, and he showed me $2,250 worth of paid tickets. I took his money, counted it, and handed him back the $750 difference between the contract price and what he had actually taken in at the door. He was stunned. He assured me that I didn't have to give him anything back, that he was good for his word and his contract. I explained that neither of us could have predicted the snow, and for him to shoulder the entire loss was just not right. He gratefully, and quickly, took the cash. It's okay to give back money to make things fair. As your career progresses and there are more layers—road managers, agents and managers—between you and the harsh realities of showbiz, try not to lose touch with what's happening to people in your name.

By the way, it also works the other way. I was playing a show at a venue in Maine, as one of three acts on the bill. The show was represented to me with a certain expected gross. The show did much better than expected, yet I was locked into the existing contract. I had no hesitation in explaining to the people involved that the circumstances had changed and that the deal was not fair now, and that my fee should be adjusted upward. They responded that a deal was a deal, and it would not change. I was most disappointed.

Fairness should be the rule. After the terms of a contract have been lived up to, it's okay to make an adjustment if both sides agree.

It's not a sign of weakness to make a little wiggle room. When people get unfairly beaten up, they either go out of business or turn vicious. If they go out of business, you have no place to play, and you know you were a party to the failure of the venue. If they turn mean, it is in response to losing so much. Both are sad.

Dangers That Await You

What makes people desperate? Three common offenders are money, drugs and sex. In the music business, there is a lot of all three, so be careful.

I ask Phil about a rumor I've heard that something happened to his guitar.

Phil tells the class, "Yeah. I left it in a friend's car on Saturday night, and when I got back from dinner, it was gone."

"Oh, Phil, I am so sorry. I am crushed that someone would be so desperate and out of control that they would take something of yours that you both need and love. I wonder about the person who would inflict such pain. Phil, what's your mental picture of the person who did this?"

"I don't know. Probably some drugged-out slug. I sure would like to find him and put some of the pain I've got back on him."

I bet. I wonder how this person views himself when he looks into a mirror. What does he see? Does he see a thief, a criminal, an addict, someone hungry enough to steal for food? Probably not.

I think we all like to believe that the person staring back from the mirror is someone who tries to do the right thing. I'm amazed by the just-apprehended criminal on TV explaining why he shot the little old lady for twenty bucks.

"She shoulda done what I told her," he might say, or some similar feeble explanation for why this terrible thing happened. It's interesting logic. "I'm not bad. The situation was bad, and I responded."

Now, are there truly evil people out there? Absolutely. However, I believe that truly evil people are a rarity, representing a minute percentage of the planet's population. The bad news is that if one of these people has their sights on you, you probably stand no chance. But, if such evil is rare, why are so many people getting ripped off, cheated, lied to and generally set upon by their fellow man? It's simple. Good people in desperate situations or driven by unwavering beliefs do terrible things. So, for self-protection, what you need to be able to do is to reserve judgment on people, and to see their desperate situations.

"Jason," I say, "Step up here for a moment. Do you mind if I use you for a little experiment?"

"Ah, okay."

"Jason, you see yourself as a good person, don't you?"

"Yup."

"In looking at you I'm sure that's true. Do you have any siblings?" I ask.

"I have a younger brother."

"What's his name?"

"Zack," Jason says.

"You like him a lot, don't you?"

"I sure do."

"Okay, class, let's pretend that I am the professor gone wild and I grab Jason's brother, Zack, and hold him hostage, and I say to Jason, 'If you don't go and mug somebody in the next ten minutes, I am going to harm your little brother.' Jason, do you believe me?"

"Yes."

"Then get out of here and mug somebody quick."

Jason is off. He runs frantically into the street, hoping for a cop, but there is none and he's running out of time. He sees two big construction workers at an ATM with a handful of fresh money.

He runs up to them and says, "There's a mad professor holding my brother hostage! To get him free, I need to mug you and take your money. Can you help me? Can you just give me your money?"

They think he's crazy and move away. Running out of time, he heads back toward the college and sees a little old lady with a purse on her shoulder.

He explains, in desperation, "There's a mad man holding my brother hostage. Can I have your purse? I'll bring it right back when I get him free."

Her predictable answer to his panicky request is, "No." At this point, Jason rips the purse from her shoulder, returns to the classroom and frees his brother—convinced that he chose the lesser of evils to resolve a desperate situation, and that with the passing of time, all would be explained, understood and forgiven.

So I say to my class, "In ten minutes, I turned Jason from a nice guy into a mugger. Is Jason a good person? Of course he is. But in spite of his goodness, a desperate situation drove him to mock criminal behavior."

Let me repeat: I believe that true evil is mercifully rare. What we need to be able to see is not the evil person, but the desperate situation.

In show business, it may be impossible to avoid working with desperate people, but if you are strong and clear enough, they will choose to go after weaker prey.

Looking Good

I used to send out a press kit after I booked a show. A nice folder and bio information, along with some glossy photos. Those days are gone. The only medium for information transfer these days is the Internet. I've started to view my website as a mini-network— the Livingston Taylor Channel: music, pictures, videos, promoter resources, links to friends, and maybe a "radio station" not only for my music, but also for the music of my students and colleagues. As the chaos of the Internet sorts itself out, perhaps these mini-networks will become the media powerhouses of the new order.

You will need to have photos, and the more the better. What makes a good promotional photo? First, it should resemble how you or your band normally look. If you use your photo to make you something you're not—sexier, stronger, with more hair (OK, that's my thing), taller, whatever—it's a bit of false advertising. When people see the real you, they will be, at best, confused. Be truthful in your promo shots. For example, it's sad for me to watch myself get older, with more lines and less hair in my recent photos. It is, however, what I am now, and it's truthful and responsible of me to represent what I am accurately. I must confess, however, I don't complain when a photo of a younger me pops up in some article.

Keep the photos tight and close. The center and most important part of a publicity photo is the eyes. Keep heads close together; pack in close and tight. If you're spread out, it's tougher for an editor to crop the photo, and crop they will, to suit their needs. Though black and white photos are occasionally used for newsprint, virtually all photographs are shot in color these days. They can always be changed to black and white by the media outlet. As I mentioned before, all photos and press materials should be available to download from your website. Keep a fistful of glossies available in case someone wants one for a wall.

I ask the class, "Who pays for the newspaper or magazine in which your pictures will appear?"

Trevor says, "The customer at the newsstand."

Tim adds, "And the people who subscribe."

The cover price of the publication contributes only a small portion to overall revenue. Far and away the bulk of revenue comes from advertisements. People pay money to get their products displayed in a publication. Let's say you own a health food store and have plunked down a few hundred bucks to advertise it in a small free flyer—which is the press most likely to be available to the early-career musician—and the flyer's editor puts a photo of a band that looks like a group of scowling biker criminals next to the ad for your store.

You'd flip! You'd call the editor or the person who sold you the space and complain. "Why is my ad running next to a photo of a band that looks like they're going to shoot somebody, then die of malnutrition?"

The editor's likely to respond, "I'm sorry, it won't happen again."

Editors would have you believe that the sanctity of editorial rights would never be subject to the economic forces of advertisers.

Nice fantasy, but I wouldn't count on it.

Smile and look relaxed in your photos. Okay, at least don't frown and scowl. Editors have space to fill; make it easy for them to fill that space with you. Keep photo backgrounds light and neutral in tone, without too many visual distractions. Nothing should take away from the faces. Avoid the temptation of goofy or gimmicky photos. Trust me, changing hairstyles and clothes will be the source of quite enough embarrassment twenty years down the road.

Laura says, "Livingston, a friend of my mother gave me this picture of you that she took in 1974."

As Laura passes the picture around, the class is much amused that their balding Brooks-Brothers-clad instructor has a heretofore-unmentioned long-haired, pipe-smoking hippie past.

At this point, I have everyone in the class pull out various IDs of themselves, including driver's license photos. The photos are the source of much amusement and speculation as to what was on people's minds when they were taken.

When my driver's license photo was being taken, I had only one thought on my mind. I wanted my picture to say, "Please don't give me a ticket. I'm very sorry you caught me speeding, and I'll be good from now on."

Can a license photo get you out of a speeding ticket? I have no idea. Probably not, but at least it was a plan, a conceptualization of where and how this photo was going to be used. Details matter; go ahead and sweat them.

The biographical information about you and your band should be clear and to the point. It should answer questions a new friend or acquaintance might ask.

"Exploding on the musical scene, direct from a pulsating cauldron of symbiotic nuclear talent cones . . . ." Whoa, stop. If a reviewer is saying that, well that's just fine, but if you are writing it about yourself, it's a bit much. Watch the superlatives. You might start believing them. "Just the facts, ma'am." Who are you, where were you born, where do you live, what are your interests? Accuracy and truth are your allies. Better to deliver more than promised, rather than less.

People become frightened that what they are is not enough, that they won't be seen, that the world will pass them by—so they tend to inflate who they are, and as a result, they stop being believable.

Please remember: Audiences are attracted to humility and self-acceptance. If you accept yourself the way you are and forgive yourself for what you are not, you will shine brightly indeed.

As discussed earlier, the access an early career has to mass media is usually through the Web, local newspapers and small radio stations.

Many years ago, I did a talk show with the syndicated advice columnist Ann Landers, and as you might expect, she gave me some advice.

She said, "Always be informative when you're on radio and TV."

Let me take a moment and explain why this is so important. People love to learn. People love receiving new information about how the world works, even when it has no direct bearing on their life. If you cannot be informative about your craft, you will wind up talking about yourself and your personal life. Personal lives are either salacious or boring, and constant conversation about yourself tends to reinforce self-centeredness. As we've discussed many times, the good career is not about you; it's about them.

Cher was recently making the rounds of TV talk shows to promote her new CD. I found it regrettable that the only questions asked of a woman who holds a lifetime's worth of show business information and experience were ones related to her personal life.

One of the problems with a lifetime of fame is that you have to struggle to get the conversation off your personal life and back to what's important: what you've experienced in your career, what you've created, and what you've learned.

Again, keep in mind that personal lives, *well lived*, are boring. Early exposure on TV may be pretty tough to get. Local radio, blogs or newspapers will probably provide your first media exposure. Either way, be ready to talk at length about your band, your music and what you're selling (CDs, downloads, concert tickets, etc.). Expect that the interviewer may not know very much about you and might well be irritated at having his or her routine interrupted to make way for you. Address the interviewer by name, making sure that the interview is not going to be edited in a fashion that will make using the interviewer's name awkward. Thank the radio station using current ID style (for example, "Magic 106.7") or newspaper name, and make the interviewer look good. The general manager of the station may be listening, and the editor will certainly be reading. Try not to answer a long question with a single-syllable word: "I understand you and your band had quite an adventure recording your last album on location in the Baja of Mexico."

"Yup." Ouch.

I write down the names of the DJs or people who call in so I can address them by name later on.

If you're doing radio, always be prepared to play live. Keep songs short, sixty seconds or so. Try to listen to the radio station you're going to be on before you get there. Get a sense of the flow of the show—hyper morning drive, shock jock or NPR. One time, I was on my way to do a morning radio interview outside Pittsburgh. I listened to the show on my way to the studio, and it was apparent that the disc jockey was running what I perceived to be a rude and, to my ears, offensive show. It was a hard spot to be in. When I got there, I had to walk a fine line between promoting my music and not participating in his audience abuse. Frankly, I never found out how well I did. But at least I knew what I was getting into in advance.

Press Agents

Laura asks, "When do press agents come into play?"

Press and publicity agents are responsible for getting current information about you to the media and putting the type of spin you want on that information. This, of course, assumes that the press and the media are interested in you. Often, people hire press agents for a short time, pay them a lot of money and get no results. It can be very frustrating. If you pay a press agent a large amount of money and beat on them, they will get you press. But if there is no interest, the attention you do get may not be the best. *National Enquirer* stories that are untrue at best, free flyers in a grocery store, and the like are not helpful to a quality career. Your early reputation will be built largely by word of mouth. Once you are on your way and have the money to afford it, if you seek more press, you can build a relationship with a small publicity agent. Try not to overpay so you don't have to end the relationship before it bears fruit. Start early and be patient. Good press takes time.

Jennifer asks, "Livingston, who normally pays for this?"

"Sometimes you can write publicity into a record deal, but remember, the artist always pays eventually. You're borrowing money from yourself."

Charlotte asks, "If the club where you're playing doesn't like what you sent out for publicity, will they put together something of their own?"

Charlotte's question is valid. Although clubs will often sift through what you send them and put together their own ads, they can only work with what you give them. In your early career, if you and your friends don't do it, chances are very good it won't get done.

As I've said before, the best exposure available for a new band now is the Internet. As we have discussed, this has become the instrument of choice for many facets of the industry. With the stroke of a key, all information about you is available to a large portion of the world's population.

CHAPTER NINE

Home Sweet Home

New York, Boston, Seattle, Boulder, Nashville, Chicago, Bar Harbor, Los Angeles, Austin. The choice of where to live can have an important bearing on an early career. Once a career is fully established, you can probably live anywhere you want. Although, for me, life in an urban area tends to offer up a palette of challenges, good and bad, that keeps the old brain hopping.

Cities offer a diversity of music partners, competing music stores, information resources and places to find an audience: bars, clubs, restaurants, theaters, streets and subways. There are places to figure out the parts of you that interface well with the people who will be paying your salary.

Boris asks, "What about New York? I think I'd like to live there."

New York City is a wonderful, exciting place with great opportunities, but it has problems. It is *really* expensive, and getting in and out of the city to go on the road is difficult. It's hard to find enough space to safely store your gear. Parking is impossible. And a handful of guitars in a three-story walk-up or minuscule elevator is not fun. True, the best is there, as well as the worst. And if you're tough enough to take it, the competition can push you to some high levels of competence.

The important thing is to live where you can sell your music, where there is strong competition to encourage you to improve, and where there are talented people (tuners, guitar repairers, recording engineers, arrangers, teachers). In short, live in or around a major city if you're planning on selling the things you create. Living in the proximity of an extended family that supports your music is a great help. Enthusiastic relatives can cook, clean, repair, schlep and store— and in general, lend a hand to the promising early career.

For me, the definition of a major city is one that has good public transportation. A public transit system gives creativity a way to get around and meet more creativity.

Boris asks, "Where does Paul Simon live? I love his music."

"I think he still lives in New York City, but the reality is that he can live anyplace he wants. So why would he put up with the hassle of New York?" I ask.

"He can afford to," says Boris.

Why else? He's a songwriter, singer and musician. He needs and wants great musicians to play with him. And remember, great infrastructures thrive in great cities. The person who creates has the most choices. The greatest strength is the creative process, the ability to make something new out of the familiar vapors that surround us. But the new creation, although wonderful, is not enough. You still have to market what you make, or it isn't worth anything. If you can't sell it, it has no value in the marketplace. It has enormous value as the expression of the human spirit, which is the most important thing, but until it finds a market, it doesn't have the ability to pay the rent.

In 1977, I took a river trip in Alaska with a man named Yvon Chouinard. He had just started a small company called Patagonia to sell outdoor clothing, but at the time he was mainly known for his many mountaineering inventions. He is a diminutive man, and on our trip, he often held his hands behind his back. When he spoke, which wasn't often, it was usually to remark that we had been lucky with the weather (a statement that was inevitably followed by pounding rain). As he had brought a number of innovations to mountain climbing, I asked him about inventing.

With a touch of resignation, he replied, "The invention is not very important. What you invent must be marketed."

Selling or trying to sell what you create, although often unpleasant and occasionally painful, is nonetheless your responsibility. If you have other people sell for you, there's a good chance they will sell you and your art in a way that reflects their taste, not yours. It's your soul with their face on it. Mmmmm.

As my brother James says, "Don't be afraid to accompany your art into the marketplace."

The biggest problem you face in hiring people to do the jobs you don't want to do is that it can put you out of touch with the day-to-day career reality. Always be ready and able to do the funkiest, most boring jobs in your career. In the young career, you often have no choice.

One time, I was promoting a record in Japan, and we had done seven straight hours of long and difficult promotional interviews—with all the questions and answers going through an interpreter. At one point toward the end of the day, a person from my record company said, "Are you tired yet?" I replied, "Are there any more interviews?" He said, "A couple more." I answered, "Then I am not the least bit tired."

I champion myself with enthusiasm, and when I hire people to work for me, I am careful about the demands I make on them. Good management requires knowledge of and respect for other people's abilities. That said, I must tell you that personally, I am not a very good manager. I tend to push at people. Because I demand a lot from myself, I demand a lot from others. It's important to remember that in most circumstances, people are already doing the best they can. I call this the "sausage principle." It is so named for an incident on the New York State Thruway.

It was midmorning, and I was driving west around Syracuse, New York. I pulled into a rest stop and went inside to get some breakfast. The service was cafeteria style, meaning one woman served eggs and toast and then passed the plate to the next person, who placed either sausage or bacon on the plate. The plate was then passed to the customer to be added up by the cashier. Pretty simple, but there was a problem.

There was a holdup at the sausage guy. He was a gangly young man—nineteen or so—and with great concentration and deliberation, he would, with a pair of tongs, pick up a sausage from the pan and one by one slowly transfer that greasy bit of food onto the waiting plate. He was so slow that a backup of four or five people had developed at his station.

With my youthful impatience, I barked, "Yo, let's pick it up a little, okay? We've got some hungry people back here."

My hope was to speed up the process. The result, however, was that it slowed dramatically. The pressure of my wisecrack caused that fellow's hand to start shaking so badly that those tongs became a blur of random motion. Find a sausage? Forget it.

In my impatience, I had failed to consider that the fellow might be doing the best he could. When my temper gets short now, I like to take a bit of a breath and remember that kid with the wiggly tongs— the "sausage guy."

Fame

Be careful what you wish for.

Many people are remarkably unprepared for success. Their fantasy tells them that fame and income will bring them familiarity and peace. They are devastated to find that their fame instead brings them isolation and loneliness. I believe this is why people at the top of their careers occasionally die. Janis Joplin. Jimi Hendrix. Jim Morrison. Kurt Cobain. Perhaps they were self-medicating—not to get high, but simply to try to feel better when the reality of their lives at the top bore no resemblance to their earlier fantasy.

This makes fame so sad. It was going to solve so many problems. If everybody knew you, you'd have the ultimate leg up. The fantasy of fame is so delicious.

I often ask my class if they've ever had the fantasy of being famous and dealing with all those who might have rejected them on the way up.

Their responses have been remarkably consistent: "I'll be benevolent with my fame; I won't need to crush them. That they didn't hitch their wagon to my rising star will cause them agony enough."

These ideas are delicious escapes from perceived injustice. Sadly, it rarely works out that way. Fame that is generated by publicity machines and television exposure, in-depth exposés, highway billboards and the like is "gratuitous fame." It turns you into a cartoon of yourself and rarely promotes your creativity. You become famous for being famous. Because you have been in their face, when people see you, they believe that they have a right to be in *your* face. They point and stare.

I was walking through a shopping mall at midday a few years ago when I saw a most attractive woman walking a path perpendicular to mine. As I slowed to admire her, she noticed me. Her face brightened considerably. Now, I'm not all that young or good looking, so that an attractive woman would brighten at the sight of me made me feel great. And then a most disappointing event occurred. After her face brightened and she smiled at me, she tapped her girlfriend on the arm and pointed at me. Sigh. Her attention wasn't human attraction, it was product identification. Now I had to worry about what I was wearing and what shopping bags I was carrying. She recognized me. I had become an image, not a person.

Now don't get me wrong. I know my job, and I know that celebrity value is part of the promotion of my art, but we need to be very careful about our private image. When I see actors complain about the intrusion of the paparazzi into their lives, I scratch my head and think, "What did you expect? You sold your soul when you allowed your personal life to be used to grind out another drop of visibility for your latest movie. You demanded their attention when you wanted to further your agenda and now you expect to turn them off? Good luck."

Given this depressing scenario, why would anybody buy into this? They buy into it because there are wonderful things that happen when you and your art are accepted. The badge of fame, once you get used to it, gives you the ability to perform your art in the company of the very best professionals out there. Trust me. It's fun making music with the best players, in great studios, with wonderful arrangers, producers and engineers. So fame isn't really an end in itself—it's a means to an end. How high can we climb the creative mountain?

Further, when people examine the kind of fame they really want, they come to realize that it's much closer to home than they thought:

- To be known and respected by your peers as a craftsperson and an artist.
- To be recognized as a dependable professional.
- To look in the mirror and see a responsible and loving sister, father, nephew, employee or boss.
- To be able to do what you love and make a living at it.
- To walk into a room of people you know and see their faces brighten because of your character.

Now that's *good* fame.

Please remember: It's difficult to observe when you're being observed. Gratuitous visibility will hurt your powers of observation. Plus, when you're ill or injured, it's very nice to be able to disappear into your cave and lick your paw until you're well again.

Think about seeing your career as a little pod. You're on a journey, and it's fun to take the trip with your contemporaries— your bandmates, your audience, your personal manager, the road crew; those who are similar ages often have similar sensibilities and worldviews. Resist day-to-day guidance from old people. Like me, they will attempt to spare you the pain they have endured. The motive is good, but the task impossible. The pain and humor of your collective innocence will be your bond as you get older.

When it comes to important life events or when you're anticipating a long commitment, definitely seek age and experience for advice. Older record company owners, lawyers, producers and teachers (in reasonable doses) are fine, with the caveat that their egos must be in check. Careers are damaged more by arrogance than naïveté.

Take Money Seriously

Making money and keeping money are wildly different tasks. When the art of your music and performance starts solving problems for people, you will start to make money. People gladly trade dollars for the relief of immersing themselves into the reality that you create.

Wide acceptance of your craft can bring you a relatively large amount of money in a very short time. In spite of what the stupid state lotteries would have you believe, a radical change in income can be so unsettling that many artists will ignore, waste or throw away this expression of people's acceptance of their work. Later, they realize they could use some of what was wasted and regret that they didn't set some money aside. Some suggestions:

Take finances seriously. This is one of the few places where mature advice can help.

Uncle Sam is your partner. Report your income and pay your taxes. An angry IRS *never* goes way. There is a statute of limitations on every crime except treason, murder and tax evasion, and you can declare bankruptcy to everyone except hospitals and the IRS. Are you getting my drift?

Let me reemphasize, Uncle Sam is your partner. This also means he should pay his share. Find—and use—every possible legal deduction.

As soon as you can afford it, own the place where you live. The tax relief and forced savings of owning a home are important.

Fund retirement accounts to the fullest legal limit every year. Tax-deferred savings are incredibly powerful given a span of forty-odd years of work.

Be conservative. Don't be greedy. Let somebody else make all the money—you make some of the money. And how *did* the Mississippi get to be a big river? It has many trickles. Finally, remember that beyond a certain point, money is a wildly overrated commodity. If money made happiness, then Palm Beach, Florida, would be known as one of the jolliest places on the planet.

Before we start performing today, I want to talk about a demo Phil gave me last week. It had nice songs, and it was good work. But I have a question.

"Phil, why did you turn your voice down so much in the mix?

"Well, I'm not that great a singer."

"Maybe you're not Luciano Pavarotti, but you sound pretty good to me."

I like to turn up my vocals nice and loud. Why? I do it because it says Livingston Taylor on the front of the CD. While I believe that I'm a good singer, I'm also aware that my voice has limitations. I try to accept what I am, forgive in myself the things that I lack, and work hard to improve the things that I have. Ultimately, realistic self-evaluation is so much more powerful than a single, isolated pocket of talent. After honest self-evaluation, use your strengths to support yourself while you work on your weaknesses. Think of Billy Joel, standing on his songwriting while he steadily worked on becoming the fine singer he is. Then there's Jimmy Buffett, who stands on his magical audience-control abilities as he works on and develops his songwriting and recording techniques (not to mention becoming a great father, husband and pilot, as well as a successful author and restaurateur). Although he may not sell as many recordings as he did earlier in his career, his current recordings reflect an ongoing growth in genre and scope and are perhaps his finest work.

"Go ahead and turn yourself up, Phil. Nothing is more attractive than self-acceptance."

In the mid-1970s, I worked with a young and talented agent. He was starting to go bald and was very concerned about it. He asked me how I thought he would look with a toupee. Having reflected on this question myself, in a moment of clarity I suggested that "nothing looks better on a human being than self-acceptance."

He paused, thought for a moment, and said, "Yeah, okay. But what about the toupee?"

Clearly, some spiritual issues are elusive.

Let's Play More

As the semester nears the end, I watch my students critique not only one another, but also the shows and performances they attend—expressing mock dismay that this class has "wrecked their ability to blindly follow a band." They now see the whole in parts: some great, some not so good.

Laura performs a simple piece on electric guitar. She makes a mistake and instantly simplifies. The rhythm stays intact. She's learned how to throw freight overboard to keep the boat from sinking. She's learned *never to sacrifice time for technique.*

Tim is the next to perform. He's been a question mark for me the entire semester. He's been very quiet, and I have no idea of how much has gotten through. He sings an Eagles song, "Tequila Sunrise." At the end of the performance, his expression is neutral, his body is still, and his eyes are observant. The class is comfortable with the stillness as they digest the performance. Tim bows slightly, signifying the end and inviting applause. An easy smile spreads over his face, saying both, "Thank you for your affirmation," and "I agree with your positive assessment." It's a perfect ending to a performance, and a gratifying moment for me as a teacher.

Applause is a gift. Receive it graciously.

Jason joins Tim, and they play a bucket and bass duet. It's different and totally unfamiliar. When a performer does something unfamiliar, an audience relies much more on body language to tell them what's going on; their posture, facial expression and physical movement or stillness provide the glue that holds the audience to them.

Trevor steps forward to perform a piece on guitar. He's chewing gum. He quietly mumbles his name and then launches into a fine piece of music. I ask about the gum, and a little fed up with my harassment and knowing he's a fine player, he snaps, "The music should be enough."

I back off. Trevor has a point. The music should be enough. And, indeed, great players can abuse themselves and their audience and still people will come. But what a favor the likes of Louis Armstrong or Kenny G do for us. They are both great *and* gracious. Not forcing the people who love them to step through an emotional swamp to get close to the genius they crave. It's true, the wrapping can't turn a lump of coal into a diamond. But the wrapping does send an early signal about what's to come.

Trevor swallows his gum and lays before us an easy, informative introduction about how his musical piece came to be. The edginess of the confrontation leaves the class. The class explodes in applause, delighted by his performance.

Jennifer sings a couple of songs, and after she's through, someone remarks that when she started, they were scared to breathe. Jennifer agrees that she, too, was scared to breathe. I remark again that performance is like a big game of Simon Says. An audience suspends their reality and enters yours. You hold your breath, they'll hold theirs. It's hard to keep their attention when they're about to pass out from a lack of oxygen.

Krystal sings a beautiful gospel ballad to end the day's class. Jennifer accompanies her on piano. Aware of their limited rehearsal time together, Krystal sacrifices optimum stage position to be close to Jennifer, knowing that if you are close together you can solve problems with each other far more easily than if you're ten or more feet apart.

After all the cynicism, pain and toughness that we spoke about earlier regarding marketing, fame and money, the quality of their performance reestablishes why we bother.

CHAPTER TEN

So Long

The last class of the semester is always a melancholy time for me. I've grown attached to my students, and I'm going to miss them. I'm having separation anxiety. Was there something that I should have said that I didn't? Did I say anything too harsh? Was I tough enough?

I want them to do well. And by "well," I mean that I want them to drift through life with minimal fear and maximum gratitude.

When we're fearful, we're self-absorbed and isolated. When we're free of fear, we're open to take in all that is around us, to be connected to the web of life. We get a big long continual drink of the universe. What fun to not know it all, but to seek wisdom, to always be open to the wonder of life in all its aspects. My most enduring wish for all of us is continued, ferocious curiosity.

I'm getting dumber. When I was twenty, I knew everything. It was the high point, the tip of my comprehension. I've been getting dumber ever since. Here at sixty, I now know a couple of things on a few subjects. But I can't wait until I'm old enough to finally know nothing about anything.

I love Thomas Edison's frustrated exclamation, "We don't know one-tenth of one percent of anything." Such wisdom!

How wonderful to observe the world without a preconceived idea or prejudice! To understand that our time here is rare and brief, and that anything that distracts from our ability to absorb is tragic. Then to be able to give back some of what you've taken in, to be of service.

My best shows are when I'm rested, wide-eyed and neutral, wet clay ready to be imprinted for the first time with the completely unique experience of a new audience. More than four thousand times onstage have taught me only one thing for sure: you can never be sure. Any preconceived notion about what a performance will bring will be wrong. You cannot know what will happen until you are at the intersection that is the show. Each performance is a brand-new ride. Occasionally, at an important or unfamiliar performing environment, my friends will become nervous for me. They will suggest performance ideas. Invariably, after a flood of thoughts, they'll look at me, smile and say, "You're not going to do any of this, are you?" To which I usually answer, "I don't know. I'm not there yet."

When I get there and it's not what I expected, I resist the urge to turn my back on my audience in any way. When it's late and they are perhaps intoxicated and sparse, and I am tired and frustrated, it's easy to blame them for my black hole. I try to remember that I work for them. They don't need what I'm selling; they buy it because they want to. The fewer of them there are, the better they should be treated. They are the only thing between me and obscurity. It's not their fault that I'm feeling desperate. They are my employer; they deserve my affection and complete attention.

"Don't Take It Out on Us"

In the early 1980s, I found myself, not for the first time, without a record contract. In 1978, through the wisdom and energy of Charlie Koppelman, I had been taken to Epic Records and had had a wonderful run that included two albums and a Top 40 single, "I Will Be in Love with You." In addition, there had been extensive tours with Linda Ronstadt and Jimmy Buffett, and shows with Fleetwood Mac, Air Supply and Pablo Cruise, as well as a large blast of TV exposure—Merv Griffin, Mike Douglas, David Letterman and *American Bandstand*, and lots of press: in general, very fine and supportive treatment by powerful traditional music-industry forces. As I did not generate the profit levels for these companies that their attentions required, by 1981 they had begun to loosen their embrace and distance themselves from me. By 1983, I was again on my own and bumping along the bottom. The dreams and fantasies had been so lofty that it made my life out of the corporate embrace seem very low indeed. I was ripe for a lesson, and someone was about to take me to school.

The class was during my second show in a small, dingy club in New York City. The lights were crummy, the sound was poor. It was after midnight, and the club was probably one-third full, and in this little dive, that meant twenty or so people. I was onstage and fuming. Oh, how the mighty had fallen. My bitterness was adding a palpable stench to what was already a pretty funky place, and yet those twenty-odd people hung in there. Was it love or stupidity? Who knew? Then came the lesson. At one point, during a pause between songs, a person in that small crowd, in spite of his love for me, had had quite enough of my attitude and decided to give me a well-deserved suggestion. Out of the darkness, in a clear, conversational voice, came his suggestion: "Livingston, don't take it out on us."

Ah! It was as though I had been kicked by a mule. Yes, I was in pain. Yes, I was fatally infected with bitterness, but I didn't think it showed. But it did. You cannot hide onstage.

Since that night, I have had occasion to look out over small, unenthusiastic audiences and turn my knee-jerk reaction of disappointment back to the memory of that night and its bittersweet lesson: the audience is not the problem. They are the solution.

Dustin asks, rather out of the blue, "Livingston, have you ever gotten a bad review?"

Suspecting a personal agenda, I probe and find that some harsh words were recently written about a band Dustin was in. I tell him how sorry I am because I know how much bad press hurts.

When the press gets ugly, it's sad and painful. Early in my career, I learned firsthand Katharine Hepburn's observation about reviews: A bad review is terrible—a good review is never good enough. As a result, after a few years, I tried to avoid the press. The damage of a bad review is much greater than the advantage of a good one. Anyhow, I was doing a show in Cambridge, Massachusetts, that was being promoted by a guy who had to be my biggest fan. He deeply and sincerely wanted good things for me. The show sold out a couple of weeks in advance, and the promoter wanted it to be a real triumph.

Unbeknownst to me, he started calling *The Boston Globe* to get them to send a reviewer to cover the show. Because he was so fond of me, he couldn't conceive that others might not feel the same way. After much haranguing, the *Globe* finally agreed to send a reviewer.

The show was, for me, a wonderful event, but as I read the review, I was devastated and confused. The writer did not reflect my post-show enthusiasm; he trashed my performance. After about a day, the confusion left and I became incapacitated by anger. Of course, I was angry at the reviewer, but I was also furious at my promoter, who was also my friend and supporter, for throwing a rock at this hornet's nest in the first place. Later on, I saw a fan who had been at the show and read the review. He seemed very puzzled. He thought I was good, yet now the review put his good feelings about me in question. Because of my own damaged condition, I was hardly in a position to be of help.

My anger lasted almost two months. Two months of deep, real pain. Mercifully, the anger subsided, and after it had, I was able to learn a great deal: When I get a bad review, I try to remember that, just like me, reviewers are doing their jobs to the best of their abilities. It feels personal. It's not. They don't know me. They are doing the best they can with the information they've been given. And, as I've often mentioned to my class, it's okay to allow their view of me to break my heart, but I try not to allow their opinion to put me in that dangerous zone of anger and bitterness. When people are uncertain about me because of what they've read, I try to assure them that, although disappointed, I didn't take it personally and that it's okay for them, along with me, to disagree with what's been written.

That said, what kind of review would be good enough to overcome my basic insecurity? Perhaps it would read like this:

Dear reader,

When your eyes find these words, I will be dead. But do not mourn me. Oh, no. For I die happy. Last night, I saw a performance that was so good I no longer feel it necessary to endure the burdens of this mortal coil and can go to my reward full and complete . . . .

Well, you get the idea. Let me repeat Katharine Hepburn's thoughts once again for good measure: A bad review is terrible—a good review is never good enough.

For my students, this last class is bubbly and exciting. With the semester over, now only holidays, family, trips and adventure lie ahead. I see them, but they look through me into an unlimited future. They are young people in a good mood. It's the best.

Lee plays a piece on his trumpet. It's good, and the class enjoys it. I have him pick it up again from the middle, and I start to sneak up on him. I move from my seat twenty feet away to within four feet of him before he notices me.

"Why didn't he see me?"

Boris answers, "His eyes were closed."

Laura adds, "He was into his music."

It's great to be entranced by your own music, but don't go into that trance until you're sure the world around you is stable enough to withstand your absence. To emphasize the point, I have a casual conversation with Boris with my eyes closed and a pained soulful look on my face. It makes the class laugh.

Laura sings two songs with Trevor and forgets to introduce either herself or Trevor. She says, "I forgot. I'm too stressed out from exams." It's a perfectly reasonable excuse, but if people don't know who you are, how will they ever find you again? Remember, your name is important.

Phil and Krystal sing a Christmas song together. The song is familiar, and the feeling between them is good. At the end, Phil's face looks worried. A worried face is asking questions: "Was I okay? Did you like me?"

Don't ask an audience to make judgment calls about you. In the main, they are good people and they'll be supportive. But, given their druthers, they would rather believe that you were good, and that you had the confidence to lead them.

Our job onstage is not to ask whether our gift is good enough but to give what we can to the best of our ability. Let someone else judge its worth. And when the audience makes its judgment, accept it.

Jason and Jennifer perform a couple of songs, including "Under the Boardwalk," which Jennifer, playing piano, doesn't know very well. She attempts to mask her ignorance with a blizzard of notes. I have her replay the song using a third of the notes. All agree that simpler is better.

Charlotte plays a song accompanying herself on guitar. The guitar part is quite hard, and as the song goes on, more and more of her attention is diverted to her guitar hand because it's *getting so tired.* Lyrics, melody and time all start taking a backseat to the burning buildup of lactic acid in the hand that is playing the difficult guitar piece. As I make a mental note to mention the building tension in her hand, she suddenly simplifies the part and the tension evaporates. Her slight smile indicates that she has, indeed, found a way to monitor herself and a way to rest.

"Livingston, it's tough when you hear something in your head and you really want to go for it."

"Yes, it takes discipline to perform. Sometimes I'll hear Beethoven's Ninth Symphony, but I know better than to try it on an acoustic guitar." You don't get points for crashing and burning. If you don't survive the battle, there's no chance of winning the war. Live to fight another day.

The semester ends with Tim playing a forceful avant-garde piece on the snare drum. Loud and raw, it's a bit of a forced march for the class, but Tim stands his ground and insists on our attention. Most agree it was a bit weird, but good.

With a lot of handshakes and a couple of hugs, the class is dismissed with the knowledge that, as alums, they are always welcome back.

Did any of my thoughts come through? Was anything I said of value?

School is expensive, and I take the responsibility of transferring information very seriously. My usual class size is fifteen people. On the first day when I explain that the job of performing is not to put out but to take in, I watch, and usually three or four of my students light right up. They get it—from the first ten minutes, they get it. They sense the freedom that's possible if you're capable of observing and reacting rather than blindly spewing your noise into the universe. It's logical and credible, and they believe it: passion with discipline. Wow.

What about the other twelve? As the semester progresses, I feel as though I get through and make strong progress with seven or eight of them. It's the last three or four that keep me up nights, searching for words that will explain and get through.

After the semester is gone, if they're ever curious to ponder what happened all that time ago, if a vague memory of the class comes into their brain but the details are fuzzy, I want them to have a place to turn. That is the reason for this book. It's okay that they're not thinking about me. They can be certain I'm thinking about them.

Epilogue, or What My Piano Teacher Didn't Tell Me

Good performance is about what you take in, not what you put out. It's about observing, absorbing and understanding the environment into which you are placing your view of the world—this is your performance. Why didn't my piano teacher tell me this when I was nine? She didn't know. She believed that being good would be enough. And when being good wasn't enough, it meant perhaps that dark, unseen forces were at work. She also believed that there was a level of technical skill or magic beyond which nothing else mattered. Actually, she was right. Magic does happen. Sadly, the chances of that technical magic being available to most who are reading this are small indeed. Only one in millions is born with the magic, yet all of us must be heard to survive.

How will we be heard? By understanding the panic that can grip us when we're faced with the prospect of failure. By being aware of the deep danger we are in when we're in that reactive, panicked state. By knowing that the fear of failure will safely resolve into the sadness of unfulfilled hope. By believing that the pain connected with that sadness must not be given away. Owning your broken heart makes you strong, and the strength gained increases your capacity for compassion. Compassion is the cornerstone of forgiveness, and the ability to forgive is the best part of being human.

Stay focused. Put your head down and take one step at a time. Expect little improvement for at least two years, a time frame that helps avoid discouragement. Each new group you face will increase your experience. The weight of accumulated experience helps dampen the wild swings in confidence that torture the young artist. You will get better. You will improve. You will find your right size.

Always perform simply enough so that you have room to watch

your audience. It is you who asked to be in front of them. Their desire for your success is heartfelt, and their affection for you is remarkably demand-free. So continual acknowledgment of their love costs little and makes you both feel great. In time, you and your audience's infatuation with each other will mature into deep mutual respect and affection. That relationship will be a warm, even light on the difficult path that people who perform must walk.

About the Author

Livingston Taylor's career as a professional musician has spanned over forty years. He maintains an intense performance schedule, delighting audiences with his unique brand of popular music, which includes mostly original repertory from his sixteen albums. In addition to his performance schedule, Livingston is a full professor at Berklee College of Music, passing on the extensive knowledge gained from his long career on the road to the next generation of professional musicians. For a look at some of Livingston's latest performances and projects, visit www.livtaylor.com.

Made in the USA
Las Vegas, NV
02 January 2023